# Rubber Pants

## Art & Recollections

**Alan Folger**

AuthorHouse™
1663 Liberty Drive
Bloomington, IN 47403
www.authorhouse.com
Phone: 833-262-8899

The views expressed in this work are solely those of the author and do not necessarily reflect the
views of the publisher, and the publisher hereby disclaims any responsibility for them.

This book is printed on acid-free paper.

All illustrations are by the author

ISBN: 979-8-8230-1924-8 (sc)
ISBN: 979-8-8230-1923-1 (e)

Library of Congress Control Number: 2023923878

Print information available on the last page.

Published by AuthorHouse 07/18/2024

authorHOUSE®

# TABLE OF CONTENTS

Crazy People in Rubber Pants ........................................................................ 1

Flint Creek . . . Through the Willows .............................................................. 2

Herters ........................................................................................................... 3

Opening Day .................................................................................................. 9

Simple Pleasures ......................................................................................... 10

Spavinaw Creek ........................................................................................... 12

Meet Mr. Trout ............................................................................................ 14

Shirley .......................................................................................................... 15

You CAN Go Home Again… ......................................................................... 17

Tradition . . ................................................................................................... 19

The Demise of Elbert Shostack .................................................................. 20

Night Fishing ................................................................................................ 23

Goose Lake ................................................................................................... 25

Jerry on the Davidson ................................................................................. 28

Rant .............................................................................................................. 29

Sight Fishing ................................................................................................ 31

Who Knew…? ............................................................................................... 32

Hey Guys…I Got an Idea ............................................................................. 34

Roger ............................................................................................................ 36

Playin' Hooky ............................................................................................... 38

Thanks .......................................................................................................... 40

Pavlov's Fish ................................................................................................ 43

Operation Redux .......................................................................................... 45

Big Sugar Creek ........................................................................................... 46

Evening Thunder .......................................................................................... 47

The Mad Mud Hopper .................................................................................. 48

The Designated Driver ................................................................................. 49

Bunnies and Goats and Bears, Oh My! ...................................................... 53

Slough Creek ................................................................................................ 57

They Made Me Do It! ................................................................................... 59

Fishing in the Snow ...................................................................................... 62

What a Day! .................................................................................................. 64

In The Future ........................................................................................................................67

The Mayflower ......................................................................................................................68

Don't Shoot Ma'm! ..............................................................................................................71

The Basswood Lake Incident .............................................................................................72

Ancient River Smallies ........................................................................................................76

Manners ................................................................................................................................77

Little Moose ..........................................................................................................................78

Marshall Fry ..........................................................................................................................80

Is it Just ME? .........................................................................................................................82

Do You Believe in Magic? ...................................................................................................83

Crow's Feet ...........................................................................................................................85

Winter Music ........................................................................................................................86

Hallowed Waters…Deserving Veterans ...........................................................................87

Redfish ...................................................................................................................................89

The Drift ................................................................................................................................91

# INTRODUCTION

The recollections I have recorded here began to take shape on a blog that I had a few years ago, when like more than a few others of my age, I thought that writing a few memories down might be of some value to my offspring at some point down the road. Turns out that recalling them had more value to me than they will probably have to my kids, and theirs.

I found that reliving my youth, and some of my more recent days on the water, gave me an appreciation for those that led me there. My Dad, my Mom, and my Uncle George – to all of them that led me to my love of fly fishing – I thank them all. And as they peer down from Heaven and read this over my shoulder, I hope they are pleased.

The family members and friends that have shared a creek bank with me could never be thanked adequately. The muddy banks of Joe Creek, the flint stone gravel bars of Spavinaw Creek, Montana's Slough Creek, and the other streams that have been my playgrounds… are who I am.

Most of all, my thanks to Shirley. My best friend, my wife…the rudder and sail that keeps this ship afloat. Without her, my adult adventures would never have occurred. Without her urging, these and dozens of un-mentioned and wonderful escapades would never have been experienced. Thank you Shirley.

And finally, thanks to my good friend and Christian brother, Dr, Robert "Bob" Stouffer, PhD, whose interest and encouragement has made this whole endeavor a reality. His editing has made the ramblings of an old man intelligible. Thanks Bob.

I will forever be jealous of Norman Maclean for penning the words, *"I am haunted by waters."* For I am, and there are no other words that describe me so well.

Most of these recollections are real, factual events…and, some…well, maybe.

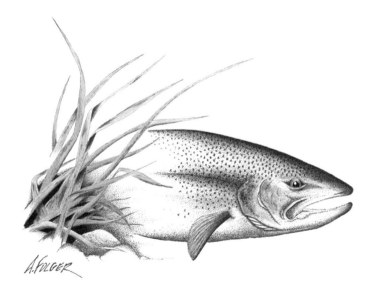

A. FOLGER

# ABOUT THE AUTHOR

From an early age, artist Alan Folger developed a love for clear water, rising trout, and God's creation. In between fishing trips he became a goldsmith and jewelry designer, a sculptor and painter, a salesman, a business owner, and author. After owning two retail jewelry design boutiques and a fine gold wholesale manufacturing company he entered the non-profit world, leading eventually to his role as the original Director of the Trout Unlimited Veterans Service Partnership. As a disabled veteran himself (Vietnam), Alan built the program to over two-hundred chapters in partnership with Project Healing Waters Fly Fishing and others, delivering the healing powers of the sport to thousands of deserving disabled veterans, nationwide.

Through his writings; his oil and acrylic paintings, and his colored pencil creations, Alan seeks to highlight the beauty of the natural world, and cause a moment's consideration and appreciation of God's handiwork by the viewer.

He and his wife Shirley reside in Simpsonville, South Carolina with their Golden Retriever, his Service Dog that answers to the name of Jordan.

# CRAZY PEOPLE IN RUBBER PANTS

I climbed the cabin steps to a front porch decked out like a well stocked fly shop. Many of the better known stores would have been envious of the display. The latest hi-tech rods, vests, waders, boots, fly boxes, landing nets, fly assortments, leaders, tippets, hats...you name it, they had it, and the guys standing around admiring and comparing their well designed display and personal accoutrements were talking about bugs...I think.

I hadn't heard Latin to that extent since I mistakenly entered the wrong, very wrong, classroom back in my high school days. I'm certain they were talking about the bugs in the stream, because I'd occasionally hear the word "trout" or "fish" interspersed in their conversations. I should add that Spruce Creek was not an inexpensive place. Harpster's Farm has private water of the highest quality, so I was certain that it must contain some very special bugs, and should they appear, my comrades were obviously fascinated by that potential.

My climb up those steps began with a very unexpected invite. Unexpected, but greatly appreciated. I was to join a group of highly-educated professionals on a famous Pennsylvania trout stream for two days of camaraderie, wine, beef tenderloin, and hopefully a trout or two. For the most part my soon-to-be friends were known to me only by their expensive professional pedigrees. Don't get me wrong...I'm not against pedigrees. I had a Brittany once that had a good one. If you ignore the fact that she couldn't hunt...never mind, she was a fine dog anyway. Fine dog, indeed. But back to my story.

It started raining that afternoon. Rained all night...not hard really, but enough rain to give the stream some color. This didn't go over well with my new pals, but it excited me. For you see, I have never been into matching the hatch. I'm into throwing big ugly things at big pretty things, and the water that was suddenly not gin clear, suited me to a T.

The next day, as they trudged along the stream lamenting the lack of bugs, I was in literal hog heaven. It was a day of fishing that I'll remember for a long, long time...but it was going to get better towards sundown.

Around 6:00pm the sun broke out as I was fishing my way back to the cabin. I could see my forlorn friends standing on the porch, sipping their Chablis when what looked like a fog rose from the water. I heard the hollering and saw each of them frantically rummaging through their vests, looking for what turned out to be....would you believe, butterfly nets.

What followed was a sight to behold. Five grown men, decked out in their rubber pants (as Shirley calls them), giggling and shouting like school-girls as they scampered across the yard to the stream, swatting the air with delight capturing, comparing, and commenting on their marvelous bugs.

I must say that the mood of that bunch improved considerably as they spent the remaining few hours of sunlight casting their "match-the-hatch" flies and catching up to my fish total for the day. I was worn out by then anyway, allowing me to sit comfortably on a handy park bench and witness the spectacle. Crazy people in rubber pants. Yes, we are.

# FLINT CREEK ... THROUGH THE WILLOWS

I like those streams that meander through the countryside with roads firmly affixed to their hips. Not so much because I'm lazy and always looking for the easy way. Well, yes, I *am* lazy, but more importantly, I'm scared to death of snakes. In spite of my general laziness however, I will hike hundreds of yards down the road to get to an easy and brush-free access point. One that doesn't require climbing over dead-falls and wondering how big the local snakes are.

Yes, I'm scared of snakes. So scared, that, if they ever make a pair of snake -proof waders, I'll have a pair and I'll catch a lot more fish. I'll wear 'em in the heat of summer no matter how heavy and un-breathable they might be, and I'll fish in places I've avoided for years. I'll do just about anything to avoid snakes.

Reminds me of a day on Flint Creek. Near the Arkansas line in eastern Oklahoma, this stretch of water was full of Kentucky's (aka Spotted Bass, *micropterus punctulatus*), and, long before the gated community plague set in, we spent many weekends camped there, wet wading and fishing for the streams plentiful inhabitants.

Flint Creek was a lazy foothills stream with deep, long pools separated by narrow rapids. At what we called the "Ledge Pool," there were no roads paralleling the creek and no trails, either, so, if you wanted to get to the next hole, there were only two choices: Stomp through the chest high bushes or wade.

Casting a tiny Lazy Ike through the length of the pool, I had caught a few bass and decided that it was time to move on downstream. The pool's outlet funneled to an unusually narrow width and was curtained completely with wispy willow branches that hung down to the water's surface. Compared to the alternative of leaving the water for what had to be the home of a thousand copperheads ...it was a no brainer. I'd wade through it.

As the stream narrowed and picked up velocity, it got deeper with each step. So deep that by the time I got to the willows, I was neck deep and barely able to keep my footing as I made my way downstream.

With my rod pointed behind me to avoid getting tangled in the tree, I reached out with the other hand to spread the willows from my face. My neck-deep venture into "willow land" went just fine for a few steps. Then it got ugly fast.

You've heard of it raining cats and dogs...even heard of it raining fish, but on that day, it started raining snakes. Yes, in the midst of that giant willow tree, I had disturbed a nest of vipers. As they dropped like a storm of long, slinky raindrops; at least two dozen of them were suddenly in the water with me...eyeball to eyeball. I ducked under water, raised my feet and let the current carry me into the next pool.

Just a few of my tormentors followed me downstream and sure enough, they were snakes; they were green, about six inches long and, of course, they were totally harmless.

Regaining my composure, I thought of what could have been. I could have opted for wading through the underbrush instead of going through the willows, and I could have been bitten by one or more copperheads and been air-lifted to the nearest hospital for painful rounds of anti-venom treatment. The nurses would have been pretty, the food OK, and I would have survived, but I would have been emotionally scarred for the rest of my life. Instead, by choosing the route through the willows, the scarring only lasted a decade or two.

# HERTERS

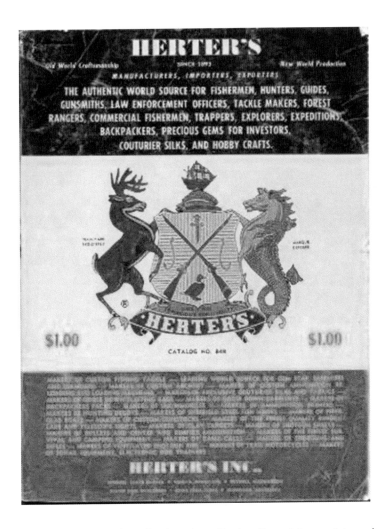

I'll have to call Orvis. A week ago, I ordered what is called a "head loupe" to salvage what's left of my eyesight. This thing from Orvis has variable magnification, and, as I am forever trying to increase the lighting on my artwork, its magnifiers with *headlights* got my attention. That and the price. I've been abusing my eyesight for decades now. Going back to the early 1970's and 1980's when I was involved in jewelry design and gemology, a head loupe was firmly affixed to my brow day and night. With all the years of close-up, highly detailed work it's a wonder I'm not cross-eyed.

Anyway, this head loupe is no good. It's no slam against Orvis...most everything they sell is first quality, and they can't be expected to be experts on everything...especially something as specialized as head loupes. The point of focus on these is off and the so-called head lights, which are nonadjustable, pointed in opposite directions away from the work zone. *(Maybe if I were cross-eyed...)* So I'm sending it back, and will continue using my old one.

Not to worry. I'm sure in a future catalog they'll be pushing an updated version. Which makes me wonder how many catalogs Orvis sends out a year. Seems like I get one about every other week, which truly tests my willpower and threatens my status as the cheapest guy on the block. It didn't used to be this way.

I was always cheap, but I never had this much temptation. Long before the days of multiple Orvis catalogs, those from Cabelas, Bass Pro, and the hundreds of other fishing gear proprietors, there was only one. HERTER'S. And you only got one a year. Growing up in a house full of anglers, the yearly arrival of their catalog was special. To see the latest and greatest gear on the market; to study each and every item and imagine its usage; to dog ear the favorite pages; and to daydream of the fish their marvelous products would catch come spring, kept us going through many winters.

As I was the family fly-tier, Dad gave me free rein to order anything and everything that I thought might be effective. To this day, I still have a number of hook assortments from HERTER'S in my fly tying kit, along with some old deer tails, floss, chenille, rusted tinsel and moleskins. *(Did you ever notice how those little skins look like miniature bearskin rugs, tanned and preserved by a tribe of Lilliputian hunter/gatherers?)*

I recently came across a familiar yellow and black envelop full of size 24 hooks. I'll probably pass those along to my grandson...at least he can see them. Since they've been in my possession for over 50 years, I doubt I'll ever use them. And another thing...you'll never catch me breaking out my tying stuff at any of the festivals I attend, 'cause the first thing I'd have to set up would be my vise. As the other tiers would be setting up their $400 Renzetti vises, I would be sheepishly setting up my old HERTER'S model...the same one you can find on EBay for just a buck or two.

I've been tying as the need arises for many years now, without one bit of improvement in my skill level. My flies were, and are, functional. I've never been accused of being an artist with hooks and feathers. Nowadays, I tie out of necessity. And my tying is an ongoing experiment in creativity. Fishing Bennett Spring in Missouri one year, I walked by a shallow pool where a good number of trout had been cleaned, and I witnessed fish gorging on the entrails, which got me to thinkin'. Later, with a tube of white silicone caulking, in a very unorthodox method of "matching the hatch," I created some pretty good replicas. Did they catch any fish? Not one, but I had a lot of fun trying. My buddy Jerry still ribs me about it, but a few years ago he too succumbed to creativity. Jerry supplied me with a selection of his "Nub Worms" which were tied with a secret product found in the automotive department of every Wal-Mart in the country. Does his creation catch fish? Yes indeed. Does it replicate anything ever seen by a trout? Not unless they are hanging out at Wal-Mart.

But I still experience the joy that comes from catching trout on a home-made fly...I remember the first one and the last one, but the in-between ones, like my vision, are a little blurred now.

## A few words regarding the photos on the following pages…

I have been blessed beyond measure…certainly more than I ever deserved. Starting with my parents, who saw to it that their boys were able to experience the great outdoors in ways that other kids our age never dreamed of.

As alluded to in one or more of my essays, Dad grew up just a few miles from a fabulous trout stream – Roaring River State Park in Southwest Missouri. Growing up, and before his service in WWII, Dad had two passions – golf and fly fishing for trout. He collected the trophies and commendations pertaining to golf, including a city championship from Tulsa, Oklahoma. He played with many of the greats of his era and even considered turning pro. His love of golf extended into his retirement, and while shooting sub-par might have been a thing of the past, his love for the game never faded.

Alas, I did not inherit either his love for, or his talent in, golf. Fly fishing was another matter. It all began with a two week camping trip to Spavinaw Creek when I was eight years old. Dad had a fine bamboo fly rod at the time which he entrusted me with. Although he never expressed regrets on that decision, he must have felt some pangs of it when I proceeded to snap in half both of his rod tips on the trees lining the creek!

Then there was Mom, the city girl that was game for anything Dad was into. As the mother of three boys, it was her passion to help provide my brothers and me with all the experiences of our youth. My earliest memories were of her and Dad sharing a stretch of water, each with exemplary skill, plying the waters for bass and trout.

There were weekend tent camping trips throughout the Ozarks, and yearly vacations to Montana, and I can't say that one was better than the other. We began, as most young families do, with tent camping, and after mastering that and all that went with it, we moved on up to travel trailers. Dad must have had three of them over the years. And as we brothers grew up, we were very successful in convincing Dad that he needed the biggest and badest engines to pull the things. (But this is about fishing and camping, so I won't be detailing our teenage car shenanigans.)

Such were my first exposures to the great outdoors.

Then I was really blessed when a young Shirley Taylor accepted my hand in marriage. She too had been exposed to camping as a child and went along with my desire to continue it. When the girls, first Stephanie and then Melanie came along, there was no question of how we would spend the few weekends that we had available as a young couple. Tent camping in all of my earlier haunts was the plan…and we did pretty good at it. To our great pleasure, our girls loved it!

We spent many a weekend at all of the places I have mentioned elsewhere, and an uncounted number of weekends at other locales that space will not allow detailing. Both of the girls loved it up until the time that they discovered boys and other girly activities.

And then, their interest in boys led to what it usually does, as both of our girl's married wonderful husbands! First was Melanie who was fortunate to marry Chad, a great young man that had very little experience in camping and fishing. Well, we changed that!

Chad took to camping and trout fishing like a duck to water. We indoctrinated him to the basics and some of the finer details, and he excelled. And best of all, when he and Melanie brought Gracie and Grant into this world, camping with Gramps and Grammy was a priority. Did I say I was blessed?

Our oldest daughter Stephanie was blessed with a fantastic marriage to our other son-in-law, Jonathan. Along with Jonathan came two young boys, John and Jacob, who soon became an important part of our family. And to our pride and joy, both of them achieved the Boy Scout's highest honor. Both became Eagle Scouts!

While our girls had outgrown their love of tent camping much earlier, they and their families did not let that stop them from joining Shirley and I on our adventures. Yes, they each had large pull-behind travel trailers which they dutifully pulled to many a campground.

So, yes again, Shirley and I have been blessed, and I hope that the following photos will give you a snapshot of the outdoor lives we have enjoyed.

# OPENING DAY

*"I'd rather eat cat poop on a cabbage leaf than participate in that goat rodeo."*

*"Dynamic always the same: arrive early, stake out a good spot, then attempt to defend it from drunken rednecks."*

*"I feel sorry for the kids that have their introduction to fishing in this kind of environment."*

Those quotes were generated and published on a very well known website recently after viewing a photograph of shoulder-to-shoulder anglers waiting for the opening siren on the first day of trout season at Roaring River State Park, in Missouri. A photo that elicited those commentaries…and for me at least, some other thoughts…

In my reading, I see lots of folks bemoaning the state of fly fishing in America. Some worry that the blip caused by Mr. Redford's movie has faded as we watch our favorite magazines bite the dust and too many of our fly shops do the same. They fear that the sport's growth is stagnant, if not declining, and that growth is a thing of the past.

One reason, and this is just a guess, for the perceived decline might be a certain snobbishness that is part of the sport that we love. A certain snobbiness that does not go unnoticed by beginning anglers.

Some sneer at those who go about their fishing in ways different than ours. For those with lesser equipment they look – yes **really** look – for the chance to introduce the term "redneck" into their commentaries. They speak of their favorite waters with reverence, flavored with a large dose of superiority. Their tackle is bought with hard-earned ego dollars, and they never fail to point out the dollars paid.

Too often we forget from whence we came. Few of us received a bamboo Battenkill for our sixteenth birthday, and our first ventures into fly fishing nirvana were not to Patagonia. In many cases, their first casts were made in spots like the one pictured above. They were for me. Literally.

But, back to the photo I referenced. I have been there. I have done that opening day exercise. It's a ritual and it's not all about catching trout. It's more a celebration that winter is coming to its end and a chance to get back on the river with old friends. Lots of old friends. Yes, they'll fill their stringers today, but, hey, it's legal, and they paid for the right to do so. I have landed (and strung) my share of those just-released stockers before the echoes of the opening siren have faded up the valley. It was my introduction to trout fishing and I loved every minute of it.

In the sixty plus years since, have I evolved to a higher plane? I certainly hope not. Yes, my tackle costs a bit more, and my destinations have been slightly more exotic, but I hope to never put down another angler because of it. Millions of words have been written about the joys of trout fishing and just as certainly, untold numbers of anglers like those that were pictured have been a part of that enjoyment.

Never assume that the guy casting a Rooster Tail to stocker trout is having less fun than you are. Do you think that guy in Patagonia holding the thirty inch brown had more fun than you did with your last bluegill? If you do, I'm sorry. You are missing the joy that got you into the sport in the first place.

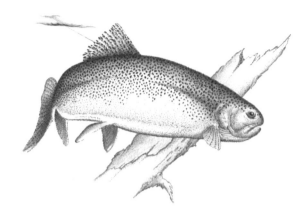

# SIMPLE PLEASURES

At the FFF Southeastern Rally last year, the always thoughtful Shirley raised her hand repeatedly during their live auction to purchase a guided trip on the Soque River in North Georgia. Ever since moving to Western North Carolina, I had seen the pictures and read the stories of the monster trout that are found there, so I was naturally thrilled with her good sense, and her persistence to win the thing. The package she won was donated to the auction by Charles Henderson of Sweetwater Anglers, and the prize was a half-day trip for two anglers on Charles' trophy section of the famed river.

It was a no-brainer that this trip was going to be son-in-law Chad's birthday present, and ever since his birthday back in September, we anticipated heading into those beautiful North Georgia mountains to meet up with a toothy, hook-jawed rainbow or two. We had a year to use the auction prize and the year was ending this Mothers' Day, so what better way to spend the weekend than packing up our families and heading to the river. And, yes, all the mothers were invited.

A few nights before leaving, I spoke to Charles, the donor of the trip, about the river conditions and picked his brain a little about what we could expect. He said if we were lucky we might get some top-water action on hopper patterns, but if not, we'd have to go deep with little nymphs. He recommended nothing smaller than 5 weights and 4x tippets. I'm likin' it already.

When we arrived at his lease – just a stone's throw from the Batesville General Store - I was a little surprised at the size of the water. This so-called "river" would have barely qualified as an Ozark "crick," but it was wild and beautiful, crystal clear, and as fishy lookin' as any water, anywhere. Charles and Chad headed downstream, and I headed up.

I hadn't been in the water but a few minutes when I noticed a trout rising no more than a good double-haul upstream of where I entered the water. As the place was too canopied for a double haul, and I can't do one on a just-mown football field anyway, I went into my excuse for a stealth mode and headed up to his position.

My dry landed perfectly, drifted over his position – and nothing happened. After three more reasonable casts, I reeled in to change patterns, as the trout rose two more times while I was fumbling through my fly box. Over the next ten minutes, I tried a couple more patterns to no avail, and finally conceded defeat. I gave him a wide berth and headed upstream with the intention of fishing back down to him with a wet. I moved upstream about 50 yards and sat down on a mid-stream rock to take in the beauty and allow the fish I had disturbed to re-settle.

As any painter would know, to make "green," you mix up a bit of blue and a bit of yellow. The shades of green that you can create are virtually endless, and thanks to an early spring with ample rains, they were all here on this overcast late-May morning. But for the patter of a light rain and the occasional crow calling out to his brethren, I was surrounded with the silence that we all cherish when on a trout stream.

Until the dogs started howling. Distant at first, the ruckus was becoming louder, closer, and more frantic as the hounds chased what was surely a 300-pound black bear toward my little slice of peaceful paradise. Of course it was a bear! What else could rile up every dog in the county? The more I thought about it the surer I was, and the larger the bear was getting. I was imagining the headline . . ."*North Carolina Angler Found Floating and Headless in North Georgia Trout Stream.*" Well, I wasn't going to sit on that rock and just let him have me. No sir, if I'm attacked and killed by a bear, I'm going to be fishing when it happens.

As the bear and the dogs changed course at the last minute - and faded off into the distance from whence they came, I was back in position to make a presentable drift with the black Woolly to my *real* nemesis, and, sure enough, on the first swing through his lair, he was on! After a few moments, I brought him alongside, slipped my forceps around the Bugger, and released him back to the river. Though certainly not of bragging size, the little 12-incher was beautiful. I continued on downstream and had a few more hits, but, other than seeing the flash of one nice fish – one very nice fish - the lunkers of the Soque had eluded me. So be it. My back was hurting, and I headed back to the truck about an hour earlier than planned.

Earlier, when we first arrived at the parking spot, in a silly mood for sure, I asked Charles if there really were huge trout in the little brown-water pond that adjoined our parking area. With raised eyebrow and a smirk, he said, "*Sure, Alan. Go have a go at 'em.*" Then we headed for the real water.

Well, after stretching out on the picnic table for a while, I couldn't resist the temptation of the pond. So here I was on a premier southern trout stream, rigging up to try out the little pond's bream population. Wham! The minute the poppin' bug hit the water, it disappeared, and shortly thereafter I had in my hand a pretty little bluegill. I won't try to convince you that each and every cast had the same result, but I will tell you that over the next hour I landed at least three dozen of the little guy's cousins.

They say that fly fishing soothes the soul. They say that it's not just about catching fish – it's about the experience. They say that standing in that clear water trout stream and soaking in Creation is good for you and your relationship to its Creator. All true. Chad and I got to do that on Saturday. I got to do that before hiking back to the truck and the pond, but, I sure am glad that I got to experience the simple pleasure of landing a fine mess of bluegills, too.

# SPAVINAW CREEK

The author on Spavinaw Creek

Got an email that got me to thinkin...why am I drawn to the clear water of mountain streams? I can start by blaming it on mom and dad. My very first memories are of creek banks. Seeing old black and white photos of me in a stroller parked on a gravel bar with dad in the background casting a fly, I have to believe that my addiction was pre-ordained. But it wasn't just trout streams back then. It was anywhere with clear water and a fish or two.

Dad used to carry one of those canvas creels, and, on the bass streams, on days when the fly rod was given up for spinning gear, he'd have one of those small minnow buckets slung over his shoulder chock full of catfish minnows. There were a lot of days like that.

Catfish minnows. We used to call them that before Christmas in 1965 when I got what is still one of my prized possessions, *A.J. McClane's Fishing Encyclopedia*. I never could figure out why we never managed to catch, or even see, a full grown version of these little black catfish, but as always, A.J. had the answer. We *were* catching full grown versions. They were Mad Toms.

Me, that Hays kid, and brother Bruce

Every night after the sun went down and the sky was at its darkest, we'd seine the rapids for them. The technique was pretty simple. With one of my brothers on one end of the seine and me on the other, we would position ourselves just downstream of dad. With a stout tree branch in hand and facing us, dad would walk quickly backwards (upstream) while doing all he could to upset the gravel with the stick. My brother and I would follow right behind him, making sure to catch everything that he had stirred up. Each pass would only be for ten feet or so, and if we were lucky, in addition to twenty pounds of flint, we'd have a minnow or two for our efforts. The seine would be laid out on the gravel bar, and, with the light of the Coleman Lantern we'd investigate our haul. While catfish minnows were the ultimate prize, we'd usually get a hellgrammite or two, a few sculpins and miscellaneous other minnows and bugs.

As long as the catfish minnow was alive, there wasn't a bass in the creek that could resist it. Hooked through the lips, we'd cast the minnow across and downstream with just enough weight to slow the swing. The minnows knew what they were in for and would do all they could to burrow under the rocks to escape the bass, and as the water was gin clear it was easy to see the bass rooting them out. One minnow...one cast...one bass. And if lucky, the minnow would survive for another go-around. Beautiful little creek bass. We called them "Brownies." There were always rumors that the creek held brown trout, and perhaps it did somewhere...maybe over toward Arkansas in its headwaters. We just figured that the locals didn't know a trout from a bass.

I've got to get back to Spavinaw Creek. I'll take a seine with me...or maybe not. Maybe I'll just give the old black Muddler a whirl. Either way, it'll be a walk down memory lane. I'll rise early at dawn and wade into the stream of my childhood. I'll splash the clear cool water in my face just like I did some sixty-five years ago. I'll wade upstream from Beatty Creek, casting toward the eastern bank. I'll kick up a few rocks and hope to see one of my old black friends. And, if the big deep pool is still intact at the bend, I'll sit and replay a few scenes form the past. There'll be a pretty girl diving in from "The Rock, "with hungry bass beneath her.

# MEET MR. TROUT

After being weaned on a steady diet of Bluegills and Smallmouths, Dad introduced my brothers and me to the Rainbow. Dad grew up in Southwest Missouri, just a few miles from Roaring River State Park, and he spent his youth casting to the ancestors of the trout we were introduced to.

Bruce, Dad, and me

Many of my earliest and fondest memories are of watching him expertly lure those gorgeous creatures with a casting stroke that would rival Lee Wulff.

I don't recall the exact year, but I must have been around 10 years old when Dad arranged my introduction to trout, and I'll never forget that summer of learning. We must have spent at least six weekends camping at Roaring River that summer, and I know that I spent from dawn to dusk slinging flies at those trout.

I believe that my first fly rod – the one that I was using – was a white fiberglass Shakespeare model with a green automatic reel. With that outfit, I caught a lot more trees, than trout. In fact, it was the last weekend of the summer before I managed to hook and land a trout. (I couldn't count the times that I would see that white, opened mouth about to inhale my fly, which was my signal to jerk it away from them.)

I remember the pool. It was the one below the bridge, right in front of what used to be the lodge. The fly was a red and yellow Wooly Worm, and I'll never forget the feeling I had.

Thanks Dad, for the introduction.

# SHIRLEY

She entered my life fifty plus years ago and she changed what would have been a wasted life of fly fishing debauchery into the life of a slightly respectable husband and father....who fly fishes occasionally.

I had great hopes of luring the beautiful young lady to my idea of a great time...fly fishing. I could just imagine us on the Firehole...landing trout after trout and being the envy of every passerby. There would be books written about us...maybe a movie. Our adventures would be legendary as we traveled the world in search of trout. But it wasn't to be.

She was up for just about anything that I was interested in, so it wasn't long before I started dragging her along on my fishing adventures. But a few trips to local streams showed me that she would never share my passion for fishing. Looking back on those days, I recognize where I went wrong...starting with our first camping trip to the Illinois River.

It had rained for days prior to our arrival. The river was swollen big time. It was out of its banks and running brown and fast, but that wasn't going to stop her introduction to canoeing, Alan style. We rented a canoe, arranged for a downstream pick-up and headed into the watery wilds of Northeastern Oklahoma.

Shirley on the Illinois River

Did I say that the river was out of its banks? Well, every sharp bend in the normally gentle stream led us through the streamside bushes and trees. And there were lots of bends. With Shirley in the front and her highly experienced white water canoeist *(HA!)* in the rear, we managed to survive the river, but not without many repeats of the following dialogue:

***"SHIRLEY ! LEFT!*** *Paddle left! Watch out for that branch!* ***NO RIGHT!*** *Hurry...****RIGHT...RIGHT NOW!***

(Insert various feminine screaming sounds here)

***"PAY ATTENTION TO WHAT I'M SAYING!*** *I said back paddle* ***NOW! LOOK-OUT! WATCH YOUR HEAD!***

(Insert more, and louder, screaming sounds here...these, directed to the rear occupant of the canoe.)

*"****IS THAT A SNAKE? !!! ALAN! THERE'S A SNAKE IN FRONT OF US!***

*"Calm down Shirley. It's just a stick."*

Some time passed before our next canoeing adventure, and, oh yeah, I forgot to mention that the river wasn't the only thing swollen. Shirley was 6 months pregnant at the time.

The actual camping was great. Growing up, Shirley had camped a lot with her folks, so she was no stranger to camp cooking and sleeping on the ground. A good camp, great food, an even better companion. I had it made. Tomorrow, we go fishing!

I had found a little backwater area where I suspected there might be a bass or two relaxing from the torrent of the main channel. As I landed a few nice Bluegills and maintained a running commentary on the many sophisticated techniques I was employing, Shirley stood patiently at my side, barely able to contain her *(feigned?)* excitement. Handing her the rod, she managed to make a pretty decent cast. And Eureka... she got a strike. Missed it! Then another strike...and another miss. More strikes followed, and despite my instructions to lift the rod and set the hook, they all avoided the hook's barb.

Her frustration mounting, I thought to inspect the fly. And sure enough, there was a reason they were missing the barb. There wasn't one. Midway up the bend, the hook had broken cleanly off...and, as she suspected, I had probably done it before handing her the rod. (No, I wasn't so insecure to have done it on purpose!) That was the last time Shirley handled a fly rod.

In the many summers since, and through the raising of two daughters, there have been lots of camping trips...in fact, Shirley instigates most of them. I'm just along for the ride...and the fishing. Her destiny was to be the "trophy" camp cook and bottle washer. And that was OK with me.

She has one fault, though. She buys tents. *"That last one (no matter how big and roomy) just wasn't big enough."* And then there's the kitchen. Everything...and I mean everything that is on the market (including the kitchen sink)...must be purchased and hauled to the campsite...even making two trips, if necessary. Setting up the camp is becoming like the set of Extreme Home Makeover, minus all the hands to help.

But what fun it is. Whether our favorite site is just a short drive from home, or a more distant spot we'll share with the kids and grandkids, we'll be there this summer. I'll be fishing. Shirley will be the pretty one tending to the camp.

Thanks, Shirley!

*The* SMALLMOUTH BASS

# YOU CAN GO HOME AGAIN...

I stepped into the cold, clear water of Upper Spavinaw Creek and stepped back in time. I waded up-stream past the confluence with Beatty Creek and cast my fly toward the eastern bank – standing in the current with as much hope and anticipation as I had so many decades ago.

Of course the Hays kid wasn't there, nor was his sister – the pretty girl on the rock. My brothers were there, though, which made it all the more special. This place is magic. The memories…ah, the memories. It is where my love affair with clear water began on a two week camping trip so many years ago.

The minute we arrived, I exited the car and walked across that blazing white gravel to put my foot once again into the stream of my youth. It was just as cold and pure as I remembered it, and, as I looked upstream, I saw that fifty-plus years of Oklahoma spring floods had not done much to alter its course.

Casting my little 2 weight against the bank, and under the trees that used to hold the brownies (as we called them), I was excited to see small bluegills and a few small bass follow the swing of my fly. In hopes of fooling them into thinking that catfish minnows were on their menu, I had tied on a black marabou, only to wish that its slinky tail had a hidden hook inside of it. They seriously attacked the tail…I set the hook with gusto…and nothing came to hand. I clipped the tail off, and of course, they ignored it.

When I switched to a yellow attractor pattern, I started catching the bream, but the bass – as wily as always – laid back and let their smaller cousins have all the fun. Eventually, I caught a few, but they weren't the familiar brownies – they were black bass. Brother Bruce, who has fished these waters often over the years since our first great adventure, told me that, just a few years back the hog and chicken pollution from upstream towards Arkansas had gotten so bad that the creek was nearly un-fishable. The resulting moss and weeds had clogged the stream, and nearly every cast meant spending a few minutes cleaning the muck from your fly.

I'm no fisheries biologist, but I suspect that the degraded water quality did the brownies in, and that the black bass, known for their ability to survive just about anywhere, had taken over. In recent years, with tougher environmental controls, the creek had returned to its former state, but without the brownies. And that's a shame, as this creek looks more like a tumbling trout stream than a backwater haven for largemouth, black bass. The fast runs that were formerly occupied by the swift water loving brownies now held nothing at all.

Still, I had a great time. A marvelous afternoon. Brothers Bruce and Tom took turns slinging my little TFO, catching many bluegills and a few bass, and I managed to catch a few myself.

# TRADITION . . .

There is a creature, *lumbricus terrestris*, which is found in or near virtually every trout stream. A trout dietician's dream food, this tasty morsel and its imitations have probably caught more fish than any other Latin named fare. Yet few of us, until quite recently, would have admitted to using them...especially the "natural", but also its many imitations.

Deep in the hidden-away pockets of your fly vest, you probably have such imitations, and, when the fish are not cooperating you have been known to use them. *Lumbricus terrestris* is an earthworm. Of course, to fly anglers, there are more popular variations which include *Paleacrita vernata*, otherwise known as the Inchworm, and perhaps the most famous of all, members of the phylum *Annelida* and the class *Oligochaeta*, the San Juan Worm.

For those of you relatively new to the fly fishing game, in days of old, no self respecting fly fisherman would have considered using these imitations...**we fished with FLIES!** Nor would we have attached split shot to a leader. We *would* have used wire-weighted nymphs, but the thought of using split shot was as unthinkable as adding tap water to a fine single malt Scotch.

Years ago, I would cuss the guys catching all of the trout using little pink rubber worms with their spinning gear. Imagine the horrors! Some were drifting these weighted worms to the dark depths of the stream with little bobbers firmly attached to their line! What they were doing was unfair, un-sporting, and downright redneck to the core!

Sound familiar?

We've come a long ways, but we still have our biases. We use "strike indicators"...just a fancy name for bobbers, and the angler without a full assortment of split shot sizes is severely limited in the number of trout he will catch. In other words, "Trout Flies" have come to mean many things. Some are made of plastic; some are made of beads; some are made from anything the imaginative angler finds at the local crafts store. And we...unlike the trout...are all the better for it.

# THE DEMISE OF ELBERT SHOSTACK

The man was a fine fisherman. Whether casting stink bait at catfish, daredevil's at muskies or delicately depositing a size 22 Quill Gordon in the feeding lane of a wary brown trout, Elbert Shostack had few equals. Today, Elbert Shostack is a babbling idiot, and this is his story.

Elbert's journey towards insanity began early in life. The only son of Elizabeth and Oscar was born into a world of big sisters. He had six of them, and in no time at all he hated all of *The Six*. Oh, how he wished for a little brother, but it wasn't to be. Pray as he might, mom and dad were finished with procreation. After all, with six beautiful and talented daughters, why keep going?

Oscar was an actuary for the Allied Insurance Company, and his idea of a good time was sitting in his easy chair and humming along with Mitch Miller, as Mitch and his bouncing ball led the national sing-along throughout the sixties. Other than that, Oscar's recreational needs were quite simple...entertaining *The Six* with Ogden Nash limericks and ridiculously stupid and unending knock-knock jokes as they worshiped at his feet...and spending his weekends building them doll houses. Elbert was lonely.

Sure, his mom doted on him, but, as for his dad, Elbert made the conscious decision in 1962 to exchange him for Ted Trueblood. And the rest, as they say, is history. The chance discovery of a *Field & Stream* magazine accomplished through a brief friendship with Ricky Peters led to Elbert's glory...and to his downfall. One of the neighborhood kids, Ricky had all the makings of a good friend until Elbert's mom got a look at him. Ricky was known to go home only when starvation was imminent, meaning that either the catfish weren't biting or the squirrel hunting was bad. But Ricky's skills as a 15 year old woodsman were legendary among his peers, and as he patiently explained to the younger Elbert, those skills were acquired through the study of *Field & Stream* and the writings of one Mr. Ted Trueblood. The problem was that Ricky's only exposure to water came from wading the creek. Ricky didn't bath, and the scabs and sores covering his appendages were enough to insure that he and Elbert's friendship would be short-lived.

And so, with the introductions made, Elbert's discipleship to the guru of the great outdoors began. After convincing the old man that a monthly allowance in cash could easily be replaced by a subscription to the magazine, Elbert began his studies. The curriculum included everything from chasing Chukars through the sagebrush of Idaho to trout fishing the country's hallowed waters. And, as Elbert grew older and opportunities to put his book learning to use came more frequently, he found that in many, if not all ways, he was indeed an honors student. Especially regarding trout fishing.

A solitary childhood led to his entry into adulthood, where he discovered to his family's disappointment that he had no need at all for female companionship. Or *anyone's* companionship for that matter. As others his age were planning families and establishing lucrative careers, Elbert stuck to his study of the classics, earning advanced degrees in Stream Reading, Bug Identification, Line Mending, and the Double Haul. His family was not at all impressed, and the cajoling phone calls from *The Six* did nothing but drive him further away. And further away he went. There was no river too far, no hunt too extreme, no woodland challenge that he was not up to.

The legend began in whispers around back country elk camps and traversed from the banks of the Mirimichi to the shores of Coeur d'Alene. Soon he was taking on the life of the gypsy...not so much from wanderlust, but more from the desire to escape the writers and fly fishing groupies that hounded his every move. The occasional article or TV spot recounting his exploits, though always questionably sourced, only served to fuel the legend and drive him further into the wilderness. Until one day, on the Middle Fork of the Salmon, when his world turned upside down.

Elbert had packed in alone, arriving just after sunset. The outpost cabin used by fire patrols was well stocked and furnished...not that he'd be taking advantage of their provisions...he was there for the bed and nothing else. Well, he might use the cook stove and supply of wood for his customary fresh trout breakfast. Sleep came easy, but not before some reflection on his circumstances.

Elbert was in his early-sixties by now. He had "been there and done that" like few before him. He thought of his long gone and distant mentor, Trueblood, and the adventures that he'd led him on. He thought of what many called missed opportunities...the lack of family and the nagging guilt that *The Six* had labored for years to burden him with...unsuccessfully. He smiled. Not just at the thought of solitude, but that he was experiencing that solitude in the Frank Church/River of No Return Wilderness, the magical wilderness that Trueblood had lobbied so hard to have established.

Note: What follows is based on the one rambling interview the wizened and gray haired recluse granted me from his room at the Idaho Hospital for the Piscatorially Insane, so its accuracy cannot be independently verified. The only thing known for certain is that Elbert Shostack never recovered.

A trout, a crazed hen cutthroat with supernatural powers, perhaps demonic powers, came to Elbert in a dream...or so he thought.

*"I was casting one of them Wulff flies. A big heavy floater, when out of the depths comes the biggest trout I ever saw. With total abandon she charges the fly and danged if she didn't jump clean out of the water and over the fly puttin' on a regular porpoise show. She clears the fly, circles around, and stops dead in the water and with a pair of bifocals stares at it...up close and personal.*

*"I reckon I was shocked, but not nearly as much as I was when she reared up out of the water, points a pectoral fin straight at me, and starts talkin'. Said she'd been waiting years for me and that now that I was here she was going to see to it that I never bothered a trout again.*

*"Well, I wasn't going to take no crap from a fish, so I asked her to please get herself back in the water and we'll get on with it. With that, she slips back down under the deadfall and dares me to try her.*

At this point in the story it must be said that Elbert was a prideful man. No, not an ego thing...otherwise he wouldn't have hid himself for so many years...it was a self-satisfaction sort of thing. Whether talking to trout or talking to himself, Elbert always had to win the argument. And to be challenged by a fish, well...

*"So there I was, waist deep in the prettiest plunge pool you ever saw...talking to a trout. And not just any trout, but one to challenge the record books. A trout that had just dared me to catch her."*

Elbert had just seen that she wasn't going to take the Wulff, so as he rummaged through his fly box, looking for the biggest and ugliest thing he had, he was thinking tactics. He thought: big trout, big fly... it had always worked before. But obviously this was going to be different. To catch a fish that talks; a fish that even knew his name; a fish that had just shown him supernatural powers, was going to take all of the skills that he had acquired over the years. Elbert secured the largest and ugliest fly in his box, *Howell's Big Nasty*, to his 4x tippet.

The cast was perfect. The drift carried it straight to the deadfall, and his nemesis, with no hesitation at all, took the fly and the battle was on. From one end of the pool to the other, she did all she could to defeat the fisherman. One powerful run led to two, then three. Wishing that he had a fighting butt on the 5 weight Sage, Elbert was weakening. As the fish hung in the current with his side to Elbert, there seemed to be little chance of moving her, but Elbert gave it his all. The Sage had to be near the breaking point, and the tippet? Well, even a 4x can only take so much.

Then the big fish started to move. Standing there at water's edge, with his rod bent double, inch by inch Elbert was bringing her in. But, as he reached for his net, the fish went back to her supernatural ways. Suddenly, the fish came up on her tail and started crabbing backwards across the pool. Just as Elbert was about to be pulled in, he was hit squarely in the middle of his forehead by the fly. The 3x long hook, though firmly secured in the fish's mouth just moments ago, was now firmly secured as a fashion statement in Elbert's brow...right between his eyes.

The big fish laughed. She not only laughed, she insulted. She made fun of his skill, his technique, and his name. She ridiculed his reputation as an angler and speculated that if he didn't get off his ass and give it one more try he would forever be known as the guy who never learned a thing from Ted Trueblood.

Elbert was shakin' mad. Sitting cross-eyed on the bank, he watched the blood inch toward the tip of his nose and plotted his revenge. *"No danged trout is gonna..."*

Composing himself, Elbert rose to his feet with determination. He checked his line for abrasions and securely fastened a new fly to the line. With trembling hands he spent little time in selecting it. After all, the fish now seemed willing to take just about anything he presented.

And she did. With her normal gusto, she slammed the offering and headed for the snag. But this time, rather than the head shaking frenzy of before, she just sulked. Then, with a burst of energy, she looked like she was trying to turn herself inside out. First spinning to the left then the right, and finally a series of frantic figure eights that turned the water to froth. The line went slack.

How she did it without fingers, Elbert couldn't say, but, when the water settled down and the fish rose slowly to the surface, there on her snout sat the fly...unattached to the tippet. The fish had untied the knot. Then she slowly circled the pool with her head out of the water, bouncing the fly like a miniature soccer ball on her nose. At the end of the lap she stopped in front of Elbert, flipped the fly high into the air, and gobbled it down just before it hit the water.

From this point on the interview became a bit deranged. As he recounted the rest of the story his words made less and less sense. There were other battles with the fish...battles that apparently included the fish speaking at various times as each of *The Six*. There were battles with the fish imitating Mitch Miller and encouraging Elbert to sing along. There was even an attempt at seduction. The fish even managed to coach Elbert in Trueblood's own voice, followed apparently by more ridicule. But Elbert never caught the fish.

According to a press report, Elbert Shostack was found a week later setting on the steps of the fire cabin. His face bloodied, his waders torn and his hands clutching what had once been a fine fly rod, he mumbled something about a large fish and a story about Mitch Miller.

Somewhere deep in the Idaho mountains a large fish swims...or maybe not. A fish that bested the best of us...maybe. And somewhere in a lonely hospital room sits a defeated man. He stares blankly at a mirror and dreams of who knows what. He raises a wrinkled hand, a hand that had held many a fine fish and brushes the long gray bangs from his forehead, revealing three of the prettiest flies you have ever seen...and cries.

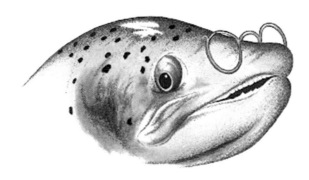

# NIGHT FISHING

Fishing in the dark. Fishing for big brown trout and not having a clue what I was doing. Wading a big river that I had never laid eyes upon...even in the daytime. Well, that's not exactly true. We got there just before dark and tried our luck along with a crowd of other anglers at a pool right next to the parking area. We had heard that the big browns were in the area spawning but I was beginning to doubt it. But we were there for the night time fishing and I was imagining that the river would come alive after sunset.

As I recall it was right around Thanksgiving...a little nip in the air. We were right below Table Rock Dam on White River. With the darkness increased, I walked away from that original pool and tried all the proven flies until I could no longer see to cast on this moonless night. And then it started. A splash here, a splash there. Then more and more. Big browns were breaching everywhere. That, or someone was throwing rocks into the river. Big rocks.

As the splashes were not right at my feet, and since I was a little leary of wading that fast water in the dark, I hoofed it back to the car to get my spinning gear so I could reach the splashes. After tying on a Rapala of about three inches, I would try to judge the distance and direction to the most recent splash. Cast after cast I would jerk at every sound, just to be safe. This went on for hours until finally a jerk met some resistance. A nice fish. Heavy with lots of fight. When I managed to pull it onto the gravel bar and get a good view of it, I was quite proud and would have been content to go home with one nice fish to my credit. If only I could have.

As I reached down to grab the big fellow, he flipped towards my hand, and yes, he placed one of those treble hooks squarely in the back of my left thumb…right behind the thumbnail. Deep into the bone. Later, we guessed that he weighed around six pounds and I felt every once of it as he continued his flopping around. I needed to get to my knife - and fast. With the hook digging in deeper with every flop, I managed to get my waders down enough to reach my right hand into my left jeans pocket and grab it. I put an end to his antics. It's a wonder that I didn't stab myself in the process. So there I was, alone and in pain, with a dead six pound brown attached to my thumb.

Finally one of my buddies, Richard from Basswood Lake fame, arrived at the bloody scene, and thankfully he wasn't carrying a pair of wimpy hemostats – he had a pair of needle nose pliers with that handy wire cutting thingy up near the handle. Goodbye trout. Now I only had the hook – minus the lure and the fish – stuck in my thumb. Off to the hospital we went.

Branson, Missouri is lit up day and night. At least it was that early morning at 2:00am. As we headed through the emergency room doors we must have been a sight. I doubt they had seen many fully outfitted fly-fishers trudging down the halls leaking water from waders and boots at that ungodly hour. Thankfully, other than us and the few docs on duty, the place was empty.

Checking out my situation, one of the docs reached in a cabinet and pulled out a huge hypodermic needle that looked more suited to turkey basting than delicate medical work. He said he was going to deaden my thumb before removing the hook. *"Whoa there doc! Haven't you seen the latest method of hook removal? The one where you get a length of cord and just jerk it out? How 'bout we give that a try before stabbing me with that thing?"*

He says, *"Sure, it's up to you,"* so I proceeded to explain the process. At least I thought I had explained it. After looping the cord around the bend of the hook…he yanked on it…I screamed…and the hook remained. I then explained that they needed to press down on what would have been the eye of the hook at the same time he yanked the cord. He tried again and I screamed again…but louder this time. Fortunately my screams had attracted another doctor, and about the time I was agreeing to be basted, he came to see what all the hollerin' was about.

This guy knew what he was doing…knew the process exactly having done it many times. He assigned two orderlies to hold down me and my arm, got a longer cord, had an assistant hold down what would have been the eye of the hook, and yanked it like he was trying to start an old Briggs & Stratton. I mean, he reared back, and, unlike the girly man doc, gave it all he had.

And the hook came out with no pain at all. Back to the river we went.

The point of the story? Scream LOUDLY if the first doctor blows it.

# GOOSE LAKE

It looked as if two very large bears, walking upright, were headed my way. As they skirted the shoreline and got closer, I could see that the "bears" were wearing backpacks.

As we came face to face, I had never seen two such filthy, bedraggled humans. Covered head to foot in soot, they said they were smoke jumpers headed back to Cooke City. They had parachuted in a few miles to our west the week before, and, with nothing more than shovels and axes had managed to put out a lightning strike fire without having to call for reinforcements. From where we were, well above timberline, I couldn't see a single tree, burnt or otherwise. They asked if we had anything to eat.

Bruce, Uncle George, and Dad

We had arrived at Goose Lake the evening before. There was a big tent set up...a canvas wall tent complete with stove...but, in spite of its hominess, my cousin and I chose to sleep outside on the bare ground. The stars were amazing, but, of course they would be from an elevation of over 10,000 feet. It was as if we had been transported to the center of the galaxy, as the Milky Way seemed to fill the entire sky. Jane, a few years older and far more studious, pointed out the constellations. All I saw were stars. If it had been a few weeks earlier, before ice-out, cousin Jane and I would have been sleeping on snow, fully zipped into down sleeping bags, and in so much discomfort the stars wouldn't have been noticed. We'd have chosen the tent.

With morning, and the smoke jumpers well fed and on their way down the trail, Mom and Dad, my two brothers, and I split up in different directions with the plan to meet up at lunch to report on what we had found. I headed for the short stretch of water between Goose and Little Goose Lakes, as Mom and younger brother Bruce headed for Grasshopper Glacier. We had heard of the glacier for years and they decided to climb the saddle between Iceberg Peak and Sawtooth Mountain to see it for themselves. Named for the grasshoppers that were embedded in the ice from a long ago storm, they promised to bring back a sample or two.

Goose Lake

Watching them grow smaller as they climbed the ridge, I headed for the little stream between the lakes. It was no more than thirty feet across. Even with the runoff going full bore it was no more than a foot deep at the deepest, and most of it was just inches deep...just deep enough to hold a trout mostly underwater. I say "mostly" underwater because, as I stood on the bank I saw nothing but shore to shore dorsal fins. A swirling, frothy mass of fish doing what fish were meant to do. If I had chosen to rudely interrupt their courtship rituals, I'm certain that I could have walked across on their backs.

These were native Yellowstone Cutthroats, but it was hard to tell that by looking at them. Because they spent the majority of their lives in the deep water of the lake under a sheet of ice, they looked more like silvery salmon. I saw that they were entering the outlet from the big lake and positioned myself on a rock ledge just above the water line to cut them off. As I watched, every few minutes a nice Cutthroat would cruise by, heading for its reproductive rendezvous. Easy pickin's...or so I thought. With just one thing on their minds though, they were very selective. It was about that time that I heard the yelling....and the hysterical laughing.

The laughing was coming from mom, and the yelling from Bruce, as he tried to stop mom from an insane rock hopping run down the mountainside. As they were climbing to the glacier, the high altitude got to her, and, as we later learned, she had a good case of Acute Mountain Sickness. Seems that one symptom of the sickness is hysterical laughter and unreasonable behavior. Of course, as she skipped down the rockslide, she was the only one laughing...the rest of us, having no idea what was wrong, were scared to death. Fortunately, the symptoms passed rather quickly when she got down to a more hospitable altitude. It's a wonder she wasn't busted to pieces when she skipped down the boulder field. They didn't attempt a return trip.

Assured that all was well, I returned to my rock perch and, through trial and error, managed to catch a few of those Cutthroats for dinner that night, tossing them behind me onto a handy spot of lingering snow.

This scenario was repeated during each of the three days we spent at Goose Lake. I don't remember too many of the other details. No idea what I caught them on or how many were actually caught...just a great memory of a barren lakeshore, high above timberline, the clear Montana sky, icy cold clear water, and a few willing trout.

The bouncing jeep ride down the trail to our base camp probably involved a stop at Star Lake for another futile attempt at the Kern River Goldens that lived there, and maybe another stop at one of the lower lakes down towards Cooke City for the Brookies...but the details escape me. So be it. These Goose Lake memories with family are enough.

# JERRY ON THE DAVIDSON

Jerry working the "D"

Jerry flew in Friday afternoon from Arkansas for some pre-Thanksgiving fishing on the "D." I had checked that morning with Davidson River Outfitters about the stream conditions, and I was assured that, although high after the recent floods, the water was clear and the fish were biting. So, after a quick "Howdy," and after unloading Jerry's gear, we headed to the river to get in a few hours of fishing before dark.

Knowing that time was short, and wanting to get Jerry on some fish as quickly as possible, we went straight to the very upper reaches of the hatchery section – way above the bridge – to begin our weekend of fishing. Sure enough, just as I was told, the water was clear…but, the catching was slow. The trout were mostly uncooperative. In the short time we had before darkness set in, we tried just about everything we could think of and managed to catch only two brookies apiece. We weren't complaining though – the trout were feisty and beautiful.

Saturday morning, fearing that the Catch and Release waters would be shoulder-to-shoulder with anglers, we headed downstream to the Delayed Harvest area to try out a stretch of water that I had never fished, and once again, we found the catching to be difficult. We covered about a half-mile of water with nothing to show for it but good companionship, and the pleasure of fishin' through some absolutely beautiful scenery.

We came upon a pool that literally took my breath away. I know you've seen those photos from New Zealand…the ones with the deep green, crystalline water, cradled by boulders strategically placed there by God just for our viewing pleasure. Well, the Kiwi's had nothing on this place! Wait…on second thought, maybe they do. We saw none of their lunker browns in the run.

After a shore lunch of peanut butter sandwiches, we went back up to the Hatchery Section, which parallels the parking lot, where I was confident we would see some fish. From many previous visits to this section, I knew there would be plenty of monstrous browns to get our adrenalin pumping. Was I ever in for a surprise. I didn't recognize the river. The floods had changed its character entirely.

Gone were the long, slow runs with their under-cut banks holding the biggest and wariest fish, replaced by a scoured-out stream with little, to no, structure. The "structure" was now placed up in the trees lining the down-stream banks. But, on the good side, the layer of silt and slime that had built up on the stream bottom; the silt that had buried, or at least partially covered the rocks underfoot, had been swept clean. It was a totally different river, and possibly a change for the better. Time will tell.

At least, we got to see some fish there. Standing mid-stream, all of a sudden the fish that weren't there, suddenly appeared everywhere…rising, jumping, slashing, and cavorting across the stream, as they partook of the Davidson's famous "pellet hatch," which only occurs when the hatchery rearing pools are flushed clean of their un-eaten *Purina Trout Chow* pellets.

As they do when this occurs, the trout paid us no mind, as they dashed around and about us, gorging themselves on the bountiful rations. A long-handled landing net and the "catching" would have been easy! But, as it was, except for one little fish caught by Jerry on Saturday, we would have gone fishless. No matter…it was a fantastic day.

Normally, after Jerry and I get together for a fishing outing, there is a story to tell…and there will usually be drastically differing versions of the story's detail. I would normally begin with an elaborate description of all the fish I caught – their size, strength, and beauty - and, out of kindness, I'd throw in a word or two about Jerry's exploits.

This time, though, the fishing didn't leave me with much in the way of embellishment material, so, I'll just say what a wonderful few days it was.

Jerry and I have shared many days on streams and lakes over the years, and some of those days were just as unproductive as these were. But, all of them are special. To think of him as my best friend, and great fishing partner, is a gross under-statement. A guy never had a better friend. May we share many more days like we just had.

# RANT

I haven't ranted about anything in a good long time, but what I just saw on TV has brought me back to my cantankerous old self. Sorry. I can't help myself. And my apologies go out to a good number of my fishing buddies who also happen to enjoy getting out in the woods to enjoy the sport of hunting.

I should start be stating that I am not anti-hunting. In my youth, I enjoyed the practice as much as anyone. Just about any game bird or animal was in my sights at one time or another. But we did it a little differently back then. A good example would be deer hunting. I did not grow up in a deer hunting mecca, and competition for game was fierce. A deer hunting trip in Northeastern Oklahoma, on public lands, was as much an adventure in not getting shot by other hunters, as it was an effort to bag a deer. I recollect one morning, in particular.

Prior to opening day, my partner Roger and I had located a woodland that was filled with signs of deer. Hopes were high as we trudged to our pre-selected spot prior to daylight on the first day of the season. As we settled in at the base of two different oak trees along a game trail, and waited for sunrise, we were amazed at the sounds we heard. There was a near constant rustling of the leaves, and we were certain that our reconnoitering had led us to a place filled with game.

However, as the sun rose, to brighten what had been a very dark night, we saw what looked to be blaze orange decorations everywhere. There was nary a tree not festooned with that color. We found ourselves in the company of who knows how many city-slickers, out for a morning of shooting. And to their chagrin, as soon as practical, Roger and I made a hasty and noisy exit from the woods. It wasn't long after that that I gave up deer hunting entirely.

Those guys, with their newly bought 30-30's, on public hunting land; guys that didn't venture into the woods more than a couple of times a year…and didn't know a deer from Uncle Gus' favorite Holstein… were not our idea of good woods-mates.

But, at least those guys were not practicing the tactics that I saw on the *Sportsman's Channel*. What I saw this evening that raised my ire was an episode titled, *North American Safari*. I only saw a few minutes of it, but a couple of minutes were enough. The guys were hunting from a camouflaged tree stand, and the first shot I saw was on a Warthog. I didn't stay enough to catch the location of the so-called hunt, but I stayed long enough to see the arrow take the beast down…as it was eating at a feed trough. A literal feed trough. And if my eyes weren't fooling me, there was a domesticated donkey feeding next to him.

What happened to the days when we actually "hunted"? Back in the day, I spent more time walking than sitting. Not that I was really good at it, but at least I was practicing the craft the same way that my ancestors did. Where is the wood-craft today? The only challenge in this sort of hunting is accuracy. If you can shoot straight, you will kill something.

Where is stalking and stealth? The only thing these modern day hunters have learned is that animals eat… and if you put out something tasty, and wait long enough, the animals will come. What happened to the "hunt" in hunting?

I have long chided my friends, and relatives, for "hunting" from a tree stand. They call it deer hunting, but I call it "ambushing." At least, most of them aren't hunting over a feed trough...with a donkey.

# SIGHT FISHING

By definition, sight fishing requires the need for pretty good eyesight. Unfortunately, mine is not, especially when it comes to the subject at hand - fishing. Having fished the streams of the Ozarks for so many years… streams where the fish really stand out because of the whitish, flint rock stream base, I have a hard time seeing the fish here in the southeast. Back in the Ozarks any casual observer, even my wife, sees them at first glance. Not so on my new home waters.

Back in the day if the fishing was poor I could narrow down the reasons. The question, *"Do you think there are any fish in here?"* was never stated. We knew without a doubt the answer to that question…why they weren't biting was the mystery. But here in the Blue Ridge, with such an assortment of rock sizes in so many shades of umber, blue, red and black, spotting fish is a problem for me, and an unproductive day usually elicits the above referenced question. All too often, I never really know if I'm casting over barren water, or not.

Fishing with Ryan can be frustrating as he stands next to me pointing at fish I can't see. *"He's right there Alan. Cast a little to the left and you'll get him."* So, I cast a little to the left (of what?) and nothing happens. I wonder if there is a fish there or not, and I'm certain that Mr. Harman is just trying to make me look bad. After all, *"The fish is right there! Any fool can see it! Why can't you catch it! You're either blind or haven't got a clue in what you are doing!"* Of course, being the gentleman he is, he would never talk like that…but I know he's thinking it. And he's right on all counts.

Phrases like, *"There must be five fish in there…all nice ones."* never pass my lips, but Ryan says it all the time. And then he goes on to catch a few of them. He can be such a show-off. I can only hope that given enough days on these waters I might be able to spot them too, and attain just a bit of "show-off" potential myself. In the meantime, I'll just continue casting to phantom fish…and hope that someday I'll find a fishing partner that's older than I am…someone that suffers from presbyopia, floaters, dry eyes, cataracts, glaucoma, retinal disorders and conjunctivitis – all at the same time.

When I find that old codger I'll know just what to say…*"Can't you see them? There's three nice rainbows – no, one's a brook – right in front of you!"* That or I'll start fishing exclusively for the Incredibly Nervous Neon Trout…the Palomino.

On hands and knees you peek over the streamside brush to check out the pool. Rising above the weeds, what do you see in the water but a large butter yellow, neon trout shouting, *"Look at me!"*

You may have been there and seen that. The Palomino trout…the most nervous fish in the stream. Everyone sees him and no one can pass up the chance to catch him. Your average rainbow, in your average stream, might go for days undetected (even by the likes of Ryan), and unexposed to the contents of your fly box. Not the Palomino. Everyone tries everything in an attempt to catch him. I'm certain that these poor trout have seen thousands of more flies than their less conspicuous cousins. On a heavily fished stream I doubt that he gets any rest at all.

In pangs of hunger, he nervously views everything that drifts by, so nervous that he won't even glance sideways, for fear of being tempted…hoping that just a few times a day, one of the morsels in the current will be edible. Reminds me of Don Knott's first character of note, "The Nervous Man," as seen on the Steve Allen Show way back when. If a Palomino could take on a human role, that would be it.

# WHO KNEW...?

On Friday morning, I began a road trip to Somerset, New Jersey, to meet with ten Trout Unlimited chapter presidents at their quarterly State Council meeting, to discuss and provide details on TU's Veterans Service Program. During 700 miles and 12 hours of windshield time, I struggled to stay awake through the monotony of the drive. New Jersey interstates are not spellbinding…or even mildly interesting.

The trip improved considerably, when, on Saturday morning, I met Rich Thomas at a convenient interstate pull-off, to follow him to our destination for the day. Rich was the TU State Council Chairman and he had promised an afternoon on the South Branch of the Raritan River as a prelude to Sunday's scheduled presentation.

Pulling off the highway and heading into the wilds of the Garden State was a treat and a pleasant surprise. The rolling hills of vibrant fall colors, the winding two-lane blacktop, and the small Rockwellesque communities that lined it, were beautiful. The many horse farms and their adjoining mini-mansions were a far cry from the apartment complexes and shopping malls along the interstate. Maybe the tag, "Garden State," is appropriate after all. Who knew?

Our first stop was in the little town of Califon, at Shannon's Fly and Tackle Shop, where I was to pick up a license for the day and meet some of the locals. This was not your local Orvis company store, but a true Catskill style fly shop that opened its doors back in 1973. Great folks and great service…service that included removing a treble hook from the hand of an unfortunate angler that stumbled in while we were there. Full service, indeed.

The next stop was a little parking area on the banks of the Raritan's South Branch. As Rich and I, along with his young daughter, geared up, I soaked in the beauty of the stream and gave thanks for the chance to enjoy such a special place.

Rich was determined to practice his nymphing techniques, while I, as usual, attached a meaty streamer to my line. As Rich worked the water along with his daughter, we leap-frogged each other from pool to pool, with no success at all. Rich thought he felt a tug or two, but I felt, and saw, nothing. As I was tying on what might have been my tenth fly of the day, Rich suggested that I move further downstream and give the "Split Rock Pool" a try. He said it was known for the number of quality rainbows that called it home. I tied on a brown Girdle Bug and headed downstream.

After surveying the water, and deciding that a position right up against the rock would give me the best shot at effectively covering the pool, I began casting. Just a few casts in - what observation, experience, and a good amount of superstition has taught me to be a good omen occurred. I was buzzed by a Kingfisher.

Me at the Split Rock

And, sure enough, on the next cast I was onto a good fish. While I was in a good position to cover the pool with my casts, I was in the worst possible position to play and land a large trout. The only way to get her to the net was to coax her upstream through a hefty current. At the end of a few good runs, and an incredible aerobatic display, the big fish – around twenty inches – was mine. YES! My first New Jersey trout.

Afterwards, Rich, being the generous host, directed me to the next hole, one called the "Measuring Pool," to try for a large brown that hung out there. I insisted that Rich give it a try first. As I relaxed, I watched him expertly work a few seams with the nymph. No luck. Then he and his daughter headed back to the parking lot – and turned the pool over to me.

As Rich headed back upstream, and, after I'd made about a dozen casts, what should appear again but the Kingfisher! Fish on! This one was half again as big as the first one, and, after a valiant fight, he was finally coming to the net. Well, maybe I needed another fly over by my bird friend – or more likely – more skill, because as he approached my net the barbless hook separated from his jaw and the line went slack. Oh, well, I was honored to do battle with such a creature.

Days end

The meeting on Sunday went well, with the attendees committing to get involved with the state's population of disabled veterans, but my mind wandered a bit. I couldn't help but being amazed at beauty of the state – and wondering if I could train a Kingfisher to be my fishing companion.

# HEY GUYS...I GOT AN IDEA

How 'bout we build a giant enclosure out in the ocean? We'll call it a park...a National Park. We'll pick a beautiful spot. A place that tourists are sure to flock to. We'll stock it with every species of ocean-dwelling creature that we can find. Both the common ones and those that are endangered. Then we'll invite the tourists. Families can swim the underwater trails that we'll establish, take pictures, and have a great time taking in the beauty and the wildlife.

It will be a masterpiece. Everyone from Al Gore to The Sierra Club will praise our commitment to ecology and the environment. It will be a true show place of sea creatures large and small. We'll have scientists monitor the various populations, and, if they see a fall-off in any given species, well, they'll just have to up the protection levels or maybe bring in some critters from the outside.

Our park will be known far and wide as the showplace of the deep blue sea. Of course, there will be some sharks to contend with, but hey, they're part of the environment too. Part of the food chain, you know. The eco-system depends on them. Of course there will be warnings signs posted from time to time if their population gets out of control, or if any of them get a little frisky. But just imagine the thrill that little Sally will have seeing a Great White up close and personal. Be careful, though, Sally. Don't feed the sharks. Might even have to close some of the under-water trails occasionally if things get out of hand.

Through our study of the parks environment, we will learn our rightful place in the grand scheme of things. We'll learn that, even with our smarts, we are no match for a Great White. Yes, there will be some deaths. But ya know, they were here first – we're in their world - and they're just doing what comes natural. If folks encounter these top predators in the park and they cause problems the authorities might relocate them to another part of the park…over by the kelp farm perhaps. And if we wake up one day and find that we are losing too many Sallys, we'll have to put up more signs and maybe even close a few more underwater trails.

Who knows, the water park environment might be so conducive to reproduction that our top predators, to expand their range, may bust out from time to time. After all, we can't really put a secure fence around the place, so the escapes will probably be pretty common. Sure, they'll harass the folks outside the park's borders, eat a few surfers and such, but, hey, that's their domain too. The outsiders will just have to deal with it. Our goal is preservation and protection of the species. The aquatic species, that is.

This is ridiculous, of course, but so is our current attitude towards another top predator. The grizzly bear. I just read that another death has occurred in Yellowstone. The second one this year, and I read not one word about the need to get rid of the Grizz. Yes, they were there first, and yes, we are intruding upon their space, but who's to say whose space it really is? Last I heard we were in charge here. (See Genesis 1:28) It continually amazes me that we, the true top predators, will allow a creature that can kill and eat us to share our hiking trails and fishin' holes. Taken to its logical conclusion, and given enough protection, these creatures, by "doing what comes naturally," will run the place.

Or take a look at South Florida, where folks move into waterfront condominiums and run the risk of losing their children to alligators. What do they do when one of these gators has the neighbor's Pomeranian for lunch? They relocate the gator. Give me a break! Kill the danged things, will ya!

Imagine yourself a city dweller. You've saved and saved for years, and you finally have the dough to buy that little slice of heaven out in the country. You move in and find the place swarming with fiddle back spiders and rattle snakes. What do you do? You kill them, of course. Even though they were there first, they are a risk to your health and safety, so you do what any right thinking person would do. What's the difference between spiders and snakes and the grizz? Or the alligator, or the Nile crocodile…or that marauding tiger in India?

So we have a problem. Do we annihilate this most incredibly beautiful large killing machine called the grizzly, or do we live with them? There are just over 600 of these magnificent animals prowling through Yellowstone National Park, and, due to a number of factors, our encounters with them are becoming more common and more dangerous. Their traditional food sources are dwindling. White bark pine trees are dying off, leaving the bears with a diminishing supply of pine nuts; cutthroat trout are at risk from climate change; and army cutworm moths are at risk, too. And there are few things angrier than a hungry bear coming out of hibernation and not finding the usual number of winter killed elk and bison to replenish his protein requirements.

What's a hungry bear to do? More importantly, what are we to do?

Just wondering.

# ROGER

We had killed more than we should have but that's the way it usually was. In truth I should say that Roger did most of the killing. I did a lot of the shooting. Not to say that I was a bad shot...I was average on most days and a little better on some, but Roger never missed. And that fact led to his ending. So right up front, this story doesn't have a happy ending.

Roger and I were friends. Not the type that hung out together to do just about anything anytime; we were huntin' buddies, and that's about all. Other than our desire to spend most mornings before school and every weekend in the field, we were polar opposites. Roger had little if any known interest in girls, fishing, or cars and could have cared less about cruisin' the strip. So we went hunting. From the 1st of September and the opening of dove season, through the end of goose season in January, Roger and I were armed and dangerous. Dove, quail, pheasants, turkey, ducks and geese, deer, squirrels, rabbits, coyotes and all manner of furry or feathered creatures would have done well to lay low. Roger was a hunter.

Roger and me

His parents were older than mine; in fact, if told they were his grandparents, no one would have doubted. His dad was retired Air Force and was a very quiet man. His mom was even quieter. They had moved to Tulsa upon retirement after a long tour of duty in the Maine woods where Roger cut his teeth on .22's and scatter guns. Roger and I were juniors in high school when we met.

During many weekends during duck season, we would travel out to the Great Salt Plains in Roger's Scout. We would drive the perimeter of the refuge looking for ponds and puddles. Situated well in the Central Flyway, the place was thick with waterfowl of every variety, and every pond or puddle was sure to hold a few of them. Setting out a raft of decoys would have worked, of course, but Roger was into stealth...so it was spot, park, crawl and shoot...and shoot, and shoot and shoot again.

It usually went something like this: Rising up over the bank, we'd spook the ducks. Up they would go, and down they would fall. I would empty my gun and figure that I hit a couple of them. Roger would do the same and *know* that he hit a lot of them. Ten shots and thirteen birds between us was not unheard of. It was that way all the time. Roger never missed, and, out of kindness, he would always give me credit for hitting a few...whether I did or not.

I always had the feeling that his family had something against grocery stores. I was sure that they lived largely on the game that Roger brought home. My family had a preference for store-bought food, so it was a given that whatever we bagged would end up in Roger's freezer. I can recall just one exception. A few years earlier Dad had bought a state of the art Hasty Bake grill. He quickly became a grill master with his steaks, roasts, burgers and chicken recipes. One day, dad stated that he'd like to try grilling a duck, so one of the fatter mallards was selected and set aside. Dad had found a recipe in *Sports Afield* that he wanted to try. On Sunday, the grill was fired up, and the duck, heavily basted with wine, was prepared. The aroma was amazing...the duck was disgusting. Roger's freezer stayed full.

We hunted together through our senior year. Every species, every season...building memories daily. Time passed. We hunted some more, and then it came to an end. We graduated from high school and Roger volunteered for the Army. I got a few letters from him. He had gone Airborne and was as gung-ho as anyone you ever knew. After setting every marksmanship record for every type of hand-held weapon the Army had, he was shipped off to 'Nam as the shooter in a two man sniper unit.

Sometime in 1968, while I was going through training in the Air Force, I was called to the commander's office. Word had come down, that while on patrol, Roger had stepped on a land mine, and he was gone.

I had wondered about how he would reenter the world when the Army had used him up. I had wondered if he could do it. Would he still hunt? Would he be even more deadly? What would he hunt? Would we hunt together again?

I found his name on The Vietnam Wall a few years ago. That tragic black wall with over 50,000 names on it. Not all were like Roger...some were supply sergeants, some were medics, some were whatever. But all were heroes. I thought of Roger a few days ago when reading about something called Honor Air...the project that flies our aging WWII heroes to their memorial in Washington. I thought of him when I read of the passengers at the Asheville airport rising to applaud a guy in uniform just back from Afghanistan. I thought about the waste. I thought about the times and the differences. I wondered who remembered. I remember Roger.

# PLAYIN' HOOKY

I got a call from Ryan asking if I could help out on Thursday. He had arranged to take some vets up to the West Fork of the French Broad for a day of fishing and as the plans were finalized he realized that he was short-handed in the "guide" category. Told him I'd have to get back to him…

Thursdays are work days around here, and business being slow as it is, taking off for a day of fishing is frowned upon. I pondered my boss's reaction to my pending request. Ryan knows that a weekend outing will find me there with bells on, but on a workday…its iffy.

I needn't have worried. The boss said OK, but he made it clear that he wasn't doing it for me or Ryan…he was doing it for the vets. *"Thanks Tim, I owe you one."*

After loading my gear and scraping a thin layer of frost from the windshield, I headed out on the ten minute drive to Davidson River Outfitters – our rendezvous point for the days' activities.

I was early of course, and spent the time rummaging through their fly inventory as if I might actually buy something. The clerk was new and was unaware that a purchase by me was highly unlikely. I inspected their selection of fly boxes; I perused their waders, and used the restroom. I was getting antsy.

Finally, I thought I'd better go back out to the car and get my gear ready. As I had already decided to use my 2 wt., I grabbed it from its bag and went to my vest to retrieve the reel. No reel. Damn, where is it! Then I remembered that I had put it in my wader bag after the last outing – but where was the wader bag?

I had brought an extra rod and reel (my 5 wt.) just in case we needed it for one of the vets, so that would take care of the reel problem, but the REAL problem was that, on this chilly day, I had to have the waders. Back to the house I went.

Thirty minutes later I was back at the shop just in time to greet the vets. There was Nancy and Harry – both in wheelchairs – and Jamie, the best crutches wielding, rock hopper that you've ever seen. To the creek we went.

The water was down a foot or more, but it was as pretty as ever. The newbie at the shop had told me that it hadn't been fished for at least a week, and I later learned that he had told Ryan that it wasn't fishing well at all.

Huh? Wasn't fishing well a week ago? Any creek, lake, river, or pond, that I have experienced, can have good days and bad. Heck, they usually have good <u>hours</u> and bad, so I wasn't worried at all. What did or did not happen a week ago was of no concern. At least we didn't hear *"You should have been here last week!"* Today was gonna be gang busters…I just knew it.

We rigged Harry and Nancy up with a couple of ten foot TFO's. Those ten footers are a great help to beginning fly-fishers, especially if they are wheel chair bound, and they began slinging weighted nymphs into the pool at the end of the meadow. Then Ryan insisted that I walk downstream to see if there were any other spots that were accessible for the chairs. I took my rod with me, of course.

The West Fork is a small stream, even when running normal, so I was pleased with my decision to go with the 2wt. and fishing downstream is right up my alley. Tying on a marabou, I gingerly entered the stream, being careful to make no waves. I saw a few 10 to 15 inch rainbows working and cast well ahead and upstream of them, hoping that on the swing they'd find the fly right at eye level. They did, and they ignored it. A few casts later one of them looked towards it, but that is all. So, I tied on a small midge dropper and headed further downstream. and two casts later I lost the entire rig in a tree. Was it gonna be one of those days, after all? Naw, keep fishing Alan, and when in doubt go with the old standby. I tied on a bright yellow Wooly.

I dunked it, I spit on it, I cussed it and it wouldn't sink. What the heck, I didn't want to spend any more time tying on another fly, so in frustration I cast it out and down and what do you know, the second it hit the water a fish slammed it…or so I thought. I felt nothing when I lifted the rod. A couple of casts later…the same thing… big splash…lift rod…nothing.

So, they like it, but why weren't they taking it? I tied on another dropper, hoping that as the bright yellow, high floating attractor got their attention, maybe they would inhale the dropper.

Sneaking into the head of the next pool I tested my theory. The third cast brought the same reaction that I'd seen in the last pool, but this time I felt the weight of a nice fish. A minute later he was in the net. He had hit the Wooly. I snapped his portrait, gently released him and decided that I should get back to Ryan and report on the lack of wheelchair access that I had found.

*"How'd you all do?"* I asked. Ryan reported that that Harry had caught a good one and that Nancy had blanked. I told him that downstream the fish were hitting on top, and true to form, Ryan repeated that they were hitting on emergers. You see, Ryan is one of those guys that tend to look at fly fishing a little differently than me. He can name any bug, tie up an exact replica, and catch more trout with it than I ever will. He is a scientist on the stream. I'm just a fisherman.

*"Emergers, huh? Well, I'd hate to see what these guys emerge into,"* I said as I showed him the neon yellow fluffy thing that they were hitting. Ryan just grinned and shook his head in disgust. "I should have known," he said.

I'll never out fish the man; after all, he has the trophies and reputation to back up his theories, but I like to do it my way. I firmly believe that confidence is just about as important as having an honorary degree in entomology, and my confidence, paired with over 60 years of experience, usually gets me a fish or two.

As the day progressed, everyone but Nancy managed to land a few more fish. This was only fitting, because on the last two outings she had out-fished everyone…both in numbers and in size. All of us are entitled to have an off day. She did, however, manage to land a nice rock. How she was able to snag and bring to net that nearly round and featureless chunk of stone is unknown. But it made her day.

Such is the way of fishing with our wounded warriors. It's not the fish (but they do help), it's just getting out there with your comrades and enjoying the quiet…the solitude…the beauty. It soothes the soul.

I beat Shirley home, and as I was relaxing on the couch the phone rang.

*"Open the garage door and help me get these groceries inside."* As I was opening the tailgate to secure the vittles, she asked, *"Did you catch any fish?"*

*"Sure did,"* I replied.

*"Did they get cold?"*

*"Not at all. Those trout are used to the cold water."*

*"I meant the vets! Shut up and get those bags into the house, smart ass. You're going to work tomorrow!"*

Reality bites…

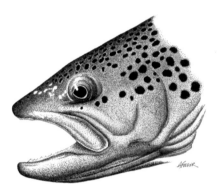

# THANKS

It's amazing that a trip that started out so badly could end up so well. Ten miles from Lebanon, my windshield wipers lost their minds. What had been a monotonous swish, swish, swish became a violent struggle for dominance, as each blade sought to overtake the other in a death-match that ended with them wedged together in a tangle, right before my eyes.

Well, at least it wasn't *pouring* rain. The final ten miles involved periodic stops to clear the view, but, eventually, I arrived for my third adventure on Big Cedar Creek.

John Bass had invited me to join him, Billy Davis, and Shawn DeJean for three days of fishing on that marvelous piece of water in Southwest Virginia. We were joined by John's intrepid guide, Bill Nuckols, and our mutual old friend, John Flannigan. I arrived just after noon on Friday.

The guys were already fishing when I pulled up to the stream. John and Billy were plying the depths of the Sycamore Hole to no avail while Bill, who had been assigned to Shawn, was trying to teach the finer points of fly-fishing to that crazy Cajun.

*"Bill, you got any more bait? I lost mine in that there tree!"*

If you have seen the TV series, *"Swamp People,"* you've heard the accent.

John Bass and Shawn go back a long ways, under circumstances that were not clear to me, but please know that Shawn would have been much more at home catching thirteen- foot alligators than he was fly-fishing on a trout stream.

I thought that I had prepared well for the weekend. Remembering that the stones were just a bit slippery from my previous trips, I had attached some lugs (sheet-rock screws) to the felt soles of an old pair of wading boots. The verdict is still out on the wisdom of that exercise, because, as I entered the water of one of the lower pools, I immediately slipped and went in to my chest. Off to a good start.

Although I was cold and soaking wet, I fought off the urge to go back to the car. I cast out my crawdad imitation and got a strong strike. A few minutes later, I beached one of the larger trout that I've ever caught. The guy completely wore me out! He would have easily gone over eight pounds. I slipped him back into the stream.

OK…now I'll go back to the car. One fish like that is enough to make my day…heck, it's enough to make an entire season!

Seeing that my fly-line was tangled, I slung it back out into the current to get it straightened, and WHAM! That first fish's twin jumped on it. After a few minutes, he was in the net. Thus began the most amazing three days of fishing I had ever experienced.

Saturday morning was cold. The temperature gauge in the car told me it was 26 degrees when I arrived back to the stream. Not a problem. Although I swore off winter fishing the year before, after a day on Duke's Creek in North Georgia, and after the two fish I caught yesterday, I wasn't about to lay out today.

But, as I dug into my gear bag I realized that there *was* a problem. Everything…waders and gloves included… was frozen solid. Yes, there was a perfectly good heater in the Super 8, but my soaking wet gear did not experience even a minute of that warmth.

I managed to get into my waders and boots, but it took nearly thirty minutes to thaw-out the gloves with my car heater.

I won't bore you with a play-by-play of the days' fishing (well, I will in a minute), but the day was magical. By three o'clock I had caught seven trout…all between seven and ten pounds. All, except one, were caught on a brownish Wooly that had two Ostrich herl pincers trailing off the tail…what is called a "crawdad" pattern.

Late in the day, I met up with John and his guide, Bill, at the low-water bridge. As John, due to a teenaged diving accident, was paralyzed, and fishing from a wheel-chair, he was fishing downstream from the bridge with his favorite fly…the Sheep Fly.

We shot the breeze for a few minutes, and I mentioned to Bill that it was time for me to tie on the Nub Worm. I told Bill that on every outing I do my best to catch a fish or two with it to honor its creator, my oldest and bestest buddy, Jerry. Bill, who happens to be a "match-the-hatch purest, laughed when I showed him Jerry's fly.

I walked a few steps down the bridge, and so as not to disturb John's down-stream fish, I slung the fly upstream. Billy, who was standing on the far bank, told me that he had seen a nice fish in the area.

Indeed there was. A Great White going after a hapless seal wouldn't have disturbed more water than the fish that Billy saw did, as it grabbed my fly and took off for the distant head of the pool. We later measured his run and determined it to be nothing less than 150 feet. He plowed through the water in a perfectly straight line, throwing a sizeable wake, before stopping for a few head shakes.

By now, Bill, having seen the action, came running with his landing net, and, as I gingerly played him back to the bridge, with one stab of his net…the great fish was mine.

Bill, who had landed many a lunker there on his home waters, estimated its weight at 12 pounds. Bill snapped a picture of this proud angler before releasing the fish for another day's battle. It was, and is, the largest trout I have ever caught.

Me and the big one!

John and Shawn, with long rides ahead of them, left early Sunday morning. Billy and I went back to the creek. We fished the lower holes, where I had done so well on Saturday, and we did just fine. Billy landed a good one, and I manage to get a few more myself.

I forgot to mention that this all occurred the weekend after Thanksgiving. God has blessed me with a great family, and a great country. My blessings are embarrassingly abundant. And, then, additionally, he blessed me with three unbelievable days to enjoy the natural world that he created. And a ridiculous number of his finned creations. Just saying "thanks" seems so insufficient.

(Oh, and one other thing: Bill, that crusty old guide – the match-the-hatch expert, asked me to tie up a few Nub Worms and mail them to him!)

# PAVLOV'S FISH

*ONCE IN A BLUE MOON.* Many of you have heard about the movie. Some might have even seen it by now. According to reviews I've read, the movie *"follows an attempt by some New Zealand fly fishers to track down what can loosely be called a 'mouse hatch.' The idea of hitting the timing just right – when an explosion in the rodent population puts the biggest trout on the feed – leads to landing some very nice fish on big mouse patterns in stunningly beautiful surroundings."*

Well, that brings to mind a story...a story that I'll tell, if you promise not to pass it on to PETA. Once upon a time, in a prior life, I worked in the egg business. A very large egg business. No, the eggs were normal sized, but they sold gazillions of them all over the good ol' USA.

As we all know, eggs come from chickens...girl chickens. For about a year, each of the girls pop out, on average, a little over one egg a day. After that, their production goes and down they aren't good for anything other than ingredients for Campbell's Soup. So they're replaced. Well, to satisfy the market demand for eggs, and to replace the worn out layers that aren't hitting their quotas anymore, it takes a lot of girl chickens. The company that employed me had millions of them, and, to get millions of girl chickens, you have to go through a lot of eggs. That meant they had to have a hatchery. And since (thankfully) science hadn't figured out a way to produce only girl chickens, the hatchery produced a lot of boy chickens, too, which were of no commercial value. Can you tell the difference in the boys and the girls at one day of age? Neither could I, but there was a family of Chinese folks that were very good at it.

On a regular schedule they would show up at the hatchery to "sex the chickens." With trays and trays of day old chicks before them, they would grab one, turn it over to inspect the "business end," and pass judgment. The girls went into another tray, and the boys went into 5 gallon plastic buckets. At the end of the day, the girls were shuffled off to a rearing facility and the boys –the cockerels – were carted off to THE POND.

A stone's throw from the hatchery was THE POND. A pond of about ten acres full of huge channel cats and bass. By now you've figured out how they got so big. For the sake of the faint hearted, I will avoid going into more details, but suffice it to say that "Pavlov's Fish" knew when it was dinner time.

Imagine a John Boat. Imagine that John Boat filled with 5 gallon buckets of lively yellow feathered vittles, and imagine that boat making 5 or 6 trips across THE POND on sexing day. I know you've seen film of an ocean feeding frenzy...well, the only thing missing were the gulls. The "Chicken Hatch" was a sight to behold.

I never did try to tie up a replica "match the hatch" fly. Didn't need to, as a yellow Jitterbug got the job done just fine.

# OPERATION REDUX

Ever since getting involved with Project Healing Waters Fly Fishing I have had the great pleasure to experience some of the finest fly fishing in the southeast. In fact, a little over a year ago, I posted a recollection entitled, "Who Needs Montana?" referring to the quality of fishing that can be had within a short drive of my home here in Western North Carolina…and I meant it! The fishing in this part of our great land is fantastic.

So fantastic that is has me spoiled. As mentioned before, when we take out the Wounded Warriors, we want to get them onto fish, and preferably big fish. Many of our local fly shops have graciously given us time on their private waters, and, without exception, the vets, and I, have caught fish. Big fish. Like I said, I'm spoiled. I got hung up on catching big, stupid fish. Shame on me.

Sunday was the cure. My good friend, Jimmy Harris, of Unicoi Outfitters fame, and I were scheduled to meet up in the Smokies for a day of fishing, and, when I suggested that we head for the trophy waters, Jimmy had another idea. Rather than test the strength of our equipment on the local bruisers, he suggested that we try something a little more soothing and serene. Jimmy wanted to try the Oconaluftee up in the park.

Right after moving to North Carolina, Shirley and I camped at Smokemont in the park, and I tried my luck on this little stream, but, being totally unfamiliar with area and the tactics required, I didn't fare very well. My Ozarkian tricks didn't cut it with these locals, and I haven't been back. Shame on me again.

Jimmy and I met at River's Edge Outfitters and headed into the park. It was a gorgeous day, with temperatures in the seventies, and, surprisingly, we had the river to ourselves. Throughout the day, we met a couple of other anglers in the parking area, but on the stream, it was just the two of us. We leap-frogged up and down the stream catching mostly native rainbows. Back at the shop, we were warned that there was a good amount of fly activity on the stream, so we stocked up on some favorite dries hoping to have a bit of top water action. But, try as we might, the ticket was down and deep.

A "back to the basics" type of day was just what the doctor ordered to cure my "big fish, easy-catchin" condition. Stealth…reading the water…fly selection…depth determination…casting accuracy…all the things that I had been missing. The largest fish would have been lucky to go twelve inches, but man, they were beautiful. The stream was crystal clear, the spring flowers were in full bloom, and the companionship was even better.

Jimmy at work

Just downstream from the Smokemont Campground, I eased my weary butt down onto a fallen log with the pretense of changing flies. Huge boulders surrounded this bend in the river, and the log was positioned, with others, on an immense slab of rock that reached to the water's edge. As I sat, I imagined this place before the white man came and turned it into a tourist destination. I imagined a campfire and an Indian brave sitting on the same slab. There might have been a few kids playing in the water, and perhaps their mother cooking a few wild brookies over an open fire. Had I been there some years earlier, I might have found an arrow-head or two, or maybe just a pottery shard. I looked around, and all I found was myself. God was good to me on that Sunday.

# BIG SUGAR CREEK

When talking to my buddy Jerry the other day, he directed me to his local Rogers, Arkansas paper and a story about one of our favorite streams from days gone by. Big Sugar Creek.

I'm not sure how we came to know about this little gem of the Ozarks, located in southwest Missouri, but for a number of years his growing family and mine spent many days enjoying its beauty and its fishing. Thanks to Jerry, the reading of the article filled my day with wonderful memories of the times we spent there.

A few years ago I learned of its evolution to become a state park, and while that designation was surely deserved, I know that should I ever return to its banks, those quiet days of yesteryear won't be possible.

In all of the times that we fished Big Sugar, I don't recall ever seeing another angler. Sure, the creek had its share of canoeists when the water level was high enough.

We usually headed upstream from the picnic area, where our wives and daughters played in the rapids just below the low-water bridge, to fish the upper reaches of the stream. This always meant that we had to negotiate the long glassy pool just above the bridge. I just called the pool "glassy," but a more appropriate term would be "Greasy," because stepping into the water with our slick-soled tennis shoes was a sure way to test our balance and coordination. We didn't have felt-soled wading boots at the time, so negotiating the algae-covered, fifty-yard-long slab of slate was the price we paid to get to the better water.

I'm not kidding – it was slick. So slick, that many days found me on my hands and knees, trying to get across it. But, it was worth it. Whether we were outfitted with our fly rods or ultra-light spinning gear, we always managed to catch fish. And some nice ones too - four and five pound swift-water bass were not unheard of, but Big Sugar's bluegills and smaller bass were great fun on light tackle as well.

# EVENING THUNDER

I hurried home from work today after a stop at the printer to prepare a few samples for the weekend's show at the South Holston Fly Fishing Festival, and another quick stop to get sheared at the local barbershop. I then hurried out to do a bit of my assigned yard work. Got that done, grabbed a beer and headed to the neighborhood pond for a few minutes of pleasure.

I figured that a few days without rain would have left the pond in good condition. On my first cast with my old standard, the yellow Wooly Worm, I had a hit. I got a brief look at her side as she rolled and thought to myself, "nice bass." But the nice bass was lazy…just plain weak. No fight in her at all. Sure enough, it wasn't a bass. A crappie. A nice one, but I didn't hurry home to catch a crappie.

The pond was dead calm and the next dozen or so cast brought nothing. I noticed a thunderhead over the horizon and decided that the barometric pressure change would be my excuse if the evening proved unproductive.

There was an aeration fountain about 80 feet out from the shore, and as I had my TFO 5 weight, I figured to test its range and see if any bass were congregating there. No luck there either. But then I saw something unusual - a swirl on the other side of the pond. Then another one…and another. Bass chasing minnows on the surface, I imagined. But even with the 5 weight, there was no way that I could reach them. I stood there a long while trying to figure out what the repeated surface commotion was all about. It continued in the same general area, so it must have been dinner time across the pond…that, or there was a leak in the pipe leading to the fountain. Maybe it was just belching air.

Returning to reality, I looked skyward and saw that the thunderhead was moving in on me, and it had gotten more than a bit turbulent. The atmosphere had turned that weird green color, and some scary looking mammatus clouds were hanging beneath the huge mother cloud. Had I been back in Oklahoma I would have considered heading for the "Hide-y-Hole," but since this was North Carolina…

Then I remembered that I had promised to grill some brats for dinner, and as grilling in the rain is no fun, I headed for the house. I fired up the grill and went inside to fry up some onions, and when I returned to check on the fire I heard the whine of the tornado siren winding down at the local fire house. (Sure glad I couldn't hear it when I was inside 'cause I hate interruptions when I'm cooking.) No more siren…no more scare…so I returned to the onions.

The brats were great, the sky didn't fall, and the bass didn't bite. But, all in all, a very nice ending to the day. Maybe I'll try the pond later in the week and chase down that disturbance on the far shore.

# THE MAD MUD HOPPER

No, the Mad Mud Hopper is not a new terrestrial to try out when the bugs return this spring. And it's not a new dance move either…though maybe it could be. My "dancing," as practiced on Saturday, was at least equal to one of my long-ago wine induced attempts at *real* dancing.

Chad and I discovered a new pool on the Davidson last Saturday. Its location will remain a secret…as if there are any secret, unknown pools on that heavily fished stream. We had the place all to ourselves, as most other anglers were tempting the pigs that hang out around the hatchery.

I hooked a beautiful brown of 15 -16 inches and as I was about to net him he darted between my legs and hung the upper fly of the tandem rig on one of my gaiters. I was wading at mid-thigh depth and it was COLD on that November afternoon. So cold, that with a wading jacket, sweatshirt, and long sleeved shirt on, I didn't want to reach down underwater to un-hook it.

Ever try to raise one leg behind you while standing in the current – in very soft sand – while holding a fly rod and net in one hand, and pathetically trying to balance with the other hand? If your knees are as wobbly as mine are…don't try it. I didn't fall in, but needless to say, amidst my hopping around contortions, the fish escaped with my dropper. It's a wonder that I didn't stomp him to death as I tried to free the fly.

Fortunately Chad, who had wandered downstream a bit, did not witness *my Dances with Trout* spectacle or I would never hear the end of it. He already laughs at what I call dancing anyway. But I do wish he had been there to see the suddenly free fish surface and laugh at me. I swear the fish had a grin on his face as his head rose above the surface for one last chuckle.

I fish…therefore, trout laugh.

# THE DESIGNATED DRIVER

I was a year late in getting my driver's license and that may have worked to my advantage. You know, I was far more mature than the average 17-year- old and, as anyone that knew me would testify, I was fully capable of driving a car full of aging anglers across two states to their favorite fishin' hole. Right. But that was my job. As the only young, driving-age relative of the afore-mentioned group, I was selected. Uncle George and his cronies had made a yearly pilgrimage in the month of June to Spicer, Minnesota for years, and a cabin between Green and Nest Lakes...a place known as Ye Old Mill Inn.

(The mill was established in 1862, and after surviving multiple Indian raids, went through numerous iterations. From its earliest role as a sawmill, it evolved, over time, into a Post Office, a grist mill, and eventually an acclaimed fishing and tourism destination. And as such, its advertisements claiming, *"Green Lake, the gem of the 10,000 lakes, with scenic interest, good fishing, wonderful swimming, beautiful beaches, and cool, clean water. It's restful or exhilarating as the need may be."*)

We arrived the day before bass season was to open. There was a guy named Bowen, a doctor named Secrist, a businessman named Coast, Uncle George, and me. We had the entire month to fish the area lakes. On the drive up I heard all the stories. Green Lake for Smallies, Nest Lake for Largemouth, and more lakes for Walleye than I can remember. As I drove, their stories...spiced with a nip or two of Canadian Club… set the stage for what was sure to be a memorable trip. A memorable trip as long as I didn't remember *everything*. It was suggested that one in my position would benefit by a selective memory when relating the details of our trip to specific family members.

Day one was a coin-toss. Which lake to try? Uncle George and I headed out on Nest to give the bigmouths a try, and the rest motored out across Green Lake. Green, which, as seen on the map, is nearly a perfect circle, and much larger than most of the lakes in the area. In addition to being a fine smallmouth fishery it was known by the locals as a great spot for ice surfing. Two guys, decked out in ice skates, and holding a sheet between them, would catch the wind and fly across its frozen surface. It sounded like great fun, but the thought of Minnesota winters and howling winds had no pull on me.

To be just a watermill wheel away from Green Lake, Nest was its complete opposite. While Green was wide-open, gravel-bottomed Smallmouth country, Nest was ideal Largemouth habitat. Multiple coves, lily pads, and tons of structure. A top-water paradise. Although I had brought my trusty Garcia Mitchell 250, Uncle George presented me with an Ambassador 5000 bait casting rig and told me it was time I learned to use it.

My first experience with bait casting went pretty well, and I soon had the hang of it...gently thumbing the spool; for the most part, I was backlash free. Casting Creek Chub Darters, Skip Jacks and Hula Poppers, we landed bass after bass. These were not Florida Largemouths. In these cold waters, with their relatively short growing seasons, a six pounder was huge. They averaged probably 3-4 pounds. We sampled a number of coves, and, as long as we could keep the Dogfish off our lines, we found the bass to be willing in all of them. The guys out on Green had no luck at all.

For the next few weeks, I guided, in turn, each of the others around Nest Lake, and spent my evenings cleaning fish. Occasional days, or at least mornings, were spent on a few of the other lakes, trying out the walleye fishing...mostly to no avail. Nest Lake was where the action was.

One evening about sundown, Uncle George summoned me to the boat for a trip up to the headwaters of Nest. He produced two small wooden and wire mesh boxes...each with a slit inner tube top, and he said we were going frog hunting. With him in the bow, and me at the motor, we set out. Now, Nest Lake was not over-run with boaters...particularly at this late hour, so I set the throttle to the max and pointed the boat to the west. About five minute into the run, I saw two frantically waving arms above Uncle George's head. *Note to Alan: When you can't easily see over the bow of the boat, never, never, never drive the boat in a perfectly straight line.* We missed the guy by inches.

Arriving at the headwaters, I beached the boat, and, with frog boxes in hand we headed into the thick weeds bordering the water. The place was alive with leopard frogs! We filled each box to the top and headed back to the cabin...zig zagging all the way.

If you ever have the chance to fish for Largemouth in lily pads, and you can get your hands on some live Leopard frogs...DO IT! I have never had so much fun fishing. Going weedless, we'd run the hook up through their lower and upper lips and aim for the lily pads. The frogs had been told by their mommas that there were creatures in the lake that would eat them, so they had no intention of leaving the safety of the pad. The frogs were well schooled, but we had other ideas. The battle for safety was the prelude to the REALLY fun part. We'd pull them off the pads and they'd scurry back on. As you can imagine, this caused a little commotion that was not unnoticed by the bass. You'd see the pads rippling as the bass converged from all directions, and, if they didn't happen to arrive while the frog was in the water they'd blast up through the pad, knocking the poor critter skyward. To see one, or sometimes two bass rocketing through the air, mouths agape all after the same frog...well, it was amazing.

Three weeks into the trip, we finally heard a good report on the Smallmouth fishing. There was a submerged gravel bar about five miles across Green Lake, and the Smallies were said to be congregating there. The next morning we filled a minnow bucket full of shinners and set off for the bar. Two or three passes across it and we had it figured out.

We'd cast a lightly-weighted minnow at one end of the bar and drift to the other. For the next hour, we caught one after the other, and none of them was less than six pounds. With each hook-up we had a Nantucket Sleigh Ride as the bass jumped and towed us away from the bar. I've yet to catch so many strong fish in one outing. Worn out and hungry, we decided that breakfast sounded pretty good, so we motored over to a boat dock and cafe to grab a waffle or two. As we arrived, we were met at the dock by a group of guys who asked us what we were using for bait. Turns out they had been watching us through binoculars as they ate *their* waffles. Well, as we ate and watched, an entire flotilla of boats headed to the bar...effectively ending our involvement in the smallmouth feeding frenzy.

Me and Uncle George

Such was my first Minnesota experience. Guiding, fish cleaning, babysitting, and some amazing fishing... and I guess I did pretty well at it, for I assumed the same duties for the next two years. Just don't ask me for more details. As Sergeant Schultz would say, *"I know nothing!"*

# BUNNIES AND GOATS
# AND BEARS, OH MY!

While the hired hand poured a full can of diesel fuel onto the stack of wood inside of the fire ring, he started talking about the bears. Said they came down about every night to rummage through the trash. Said there were a number of dens up the mountain, and, a year or two ago, one of the den mates came to work for him. Strange fellow he was. Said the bear worked out OK but smelled pretty bad.

We were at a campground that shall remain nameless, lest I be served a court summons at a future date and accused of slandering the joint. Of course, I'll have a good number of witnesses to testify to the truth of my claims…so no worries.

It so happened that this unnamed place was proud of its conservation reputation. Their campground brochure was loaded with platitudes about their back - to - nature philosophy and their love for the land. Their organic garden, their single Holstein cow – which if you timed your visit just right – could be milked by any of the campers. They also had a herd of bunny rabbits and goats, which surely testified to their eco-living commitment. As further proof, their bear dining hall was perfectly suited to serve the gastronomic needs of the bears. Their open topped trash enclosure backed up to the slope where the dens were said to be, making for an easy dumpster diving entry. And as proof, the path up the slope was littered with the evidence. Yessir, the proprietors of this place had a true love for the animals. No bear would go hungry.

National holidays and family camping have become a tradition around here, and this time we were in the deepest woods of the North Georgia Mountains. Chad had found the place on the web – a "retreat center" with full hook-ups, animal petting, a trout stream you couldn't fish in, and a spring-fed trout pond where you could. We set up our tent between our two daughters' campers and wondered aloud why anyone in their right mind would call this wall-to-wall RV experience "camping." Oh well, Chad and I were a little familiar with the surrounding waters, and planned to spend a good amount of time away from this RV parking lot. That "good amount of time" began on Saturday morning when we motored down to the quaint Bavarian village of Helen, Georgia, stopping in to see our buddies at Unicoi Outfitters to get the latest fishing reports.

They recommended the upper Chattahoochee, but getting there was going to take a little longer than usual. The tornado that came through on Thursday afternoon – the one we heard about on the Weather Channel that delayed our leaving home by a day – had downed a good number of trees on the Forest Service road we would have normally taken, so we had to go the long way.

Five miles of bone-jarring switchbacks led us to the headwaters to the Chattahoochee River. Little more than a small creek, 150 miles as the crow flies, and with who knows how many tributaries later, this pristine, tiny trout stream would turn into a wide and brown colored river near Chad and Melanie's Columbus, Georgia home.

The fishing was a bit different than the available fishing back at the campground. Check out this warning they had posted at the "keep and pay for what you catch" trout pond. So releasing fish kills them? In fairness, it probably does, if you hook them deep enough with a night crawler. Six bucks a pound, if you please!

But I digress…Chad and I managed to catch and release a good number of native trout, and the best color was yellow. I know… surprise, surprise. Hey, if it works for ya, why change? I stuck with a yellow hackled wooly with a black chenille body and a black marabou tail, and Chad's fly of choice was about the same. We probably spent around three hours on the stream, and the ride back to camp had us wishing for those NASCAR carbon fiber seats and HANS Devices to protect us from the whiplash treatment of the weathered and well-rutted road.

The next morning Chad - along with Stephanie's fiancé Jonathan, and his young boys, John and Jacob, were able to convince me that these old knees could climb the mountain behind the camp. They theorized that if we climbed high enough we were sure to find some native brookies. I wasn't about to wimp out, although midway up that first ledge, I threatened to. Glad I didn't.

Near the top we came across the remains of what might have been a water-wheel. Nothing was left but the concrete supports, and, looking at the log reinforced channel above it, I was certain that we had happened upon what had once been some sort of water-powered mill. That is, until we saw this sign.

The intricately place bank retainers – so far up the mountain and laid with such obvious care and planning – showed that some dedicated and REAL conservationist had done some very back-breaking work to ensure that our beloved little brookies had a place to thrive. Thank you, Trout Unlimited.

Right after we saw the sign, Chad proceeded to catch one of the creeks' beauties.

Unfortunately, that was the only one landed, but to be in their presence; to walk the unspoiled forest, and to practice our Joe Humphries bow-and-arrow casts…we were in brookie heaven.

Meanwhile, back at the campground, around sundown, the old lady that owned the place was on patrol. Traveling from one campsite to the next on her golf cart, she interrogated everyone about their numbers – kids, dogs, guests, tents and vehicles – all under the guise of striking up a friendly conversation. Through her accusatory interrogations, she managed to collect a few extra bucks from everyone, and, if you questioned her arithmetic or her logic, her standard response was…"*You just don't understand. We are conservationists!*" There were charges for everything, including the grass seed she would have to lay down after our tent was removed. No wonder her so-called campground was the only one with vacancies on this holiday weekend. She'll have a few more next year.

On Sunday, everyone but Shirley and I took off for another hike. Deciding to take a short-cut, they - meaning Melanie and Chad and our grandkids, Gracie and Grant along with Stephanie and her fiancé and his two boys, Jon and Jacob – left the main trail and headed through the brush. After passing many caves and wondering where the bears were, they had a great time playing at the foot of a number of waterfalls.

The kids

Eventually they came back to the trail, going in a downhill direction. As they descended back towards civilization, they came across some crime scene tape and a sign posted to a tree that anyone climbing the trail in the right direction would have seen. It read: *"Caution! There is fresh bear sign all along this trail. Be aware of your surroundings and make noise, talking, etc. if you choose to hike."*

All in all, it was a great holiday spent with family. Chad and I fished some incredible waters; we ate some great food; and we enjoyed each other's company. We avoided the tornado and survived the harassment of our hosts. We even managed to avoid the bears. Will we go back? Not to the place I promised not to mention, but to the area? Absolutely.

# SLOUGH CREEK

*"The creek was really down and clearer than I have ever seen it. They had a warm spring up here. About halfway up the meadow I spooked a nice fish - the largest I've seen today. He swam downstream about twenty yards and I eased back into the grass to let him get back to his chosen position. I waited about five minutes and walked downstream of him. I made a couple of false casts upstream and dropped the Adams about three feet above him. He took on the third cast and made a strong run downstream. My reel was really singing..."*

The wording above came verbatim from my fishing journal dated July 28, 1962. We spent many days, over many years, fishing the upper meadows of Slough Creek and many nights since, in that hazy period just before nodding off, I've replayed this episode and many more like it.

I'm told that the creek is pretty much the same today as yesterday, with the exception of the traffic it gets. Our days of fishing the upper meadows were rarely interrupted by the presence of other anglers. It was just us and the mosquitoes, with the occasional interruption by the buttery, red-jawed denizens of its waters.

The journal entry continues:

*"I had to follow him downstream, not because of lack of line, but there was a steep bank where I hooked him, and I had to find a place to land him. He fought me for about 5 minutes and I landed him on a mud bank. The fish was bigger than I thought. It measured 16 1/2 inches and weighed 3 1/4 pounds, the largest fish of the day. The rest of the family fished the Lamar down from the ranger station and brought home 7 fish."*

Later, in another year, on this same stream, I had one of those hair-on-the-back-of-the-neck experiences. As soon as the car was parked at the campground, I headed up the trail to the 1st Meadow. Back at our base in Cooke City, we had heard many stories about the bears, so, as usual, I was a little nervous. We had heard that the area had more grizzlies than anyplace else in the lower 48.

A few days before, on an outing to West Yellowstone, we had seen "The Grizz" at relatively close range. Pulling up to the edge of the city dump just before sundown, we saw at least twenty black bears of all sizes rooting through the garbage when, all of a sudden, in unison, they all stood on their hind legs and looked off in the same direction. Sniffing the air, again in unison, they hightailed it out of there. Up the hill came "Ole Slewfoot," the bear made famous by the Craighead brothers, and none of the black bears wanted anything to do with that swaggering monster, or the other grizzlies that followed along. As we watched from the safety of the car, we gained a new level of respect for the power and grace of those animals as they sparred with one another over the remains of some happy family's dinner.

The trail from the campground was easy to follow. We were told that it ended at a place named Silvertip Ranch. Wary of the bears, I made as much noise as I could, whistling and singing the pop hits of the day. I saw bear sign a time or two but never saw the perpetrators. One of the rangers back in Cooke had made matters worse by telling us about the buffalos. He said they were far more dangerous and totally unpredictable. I was on guard for sure.

At one point along the canyon the trail came pretty close to the stream...close enough that I could hear the water. Not one to pass up a trout or two, I had to give it a try. I left the trail and headed through the pines to the stream. Getting closer, it was clear that the water was below the level that I was on, so as I neared the water I dropped to a crawl to avoid spooking any trout that might be waiting. As I neared the bank I could see the far side of a very nice pool below the drop-off. Excitement was in the air when I inched toward the edge and just as I peered over...moose antlers were in the air also. And right in front of my face.

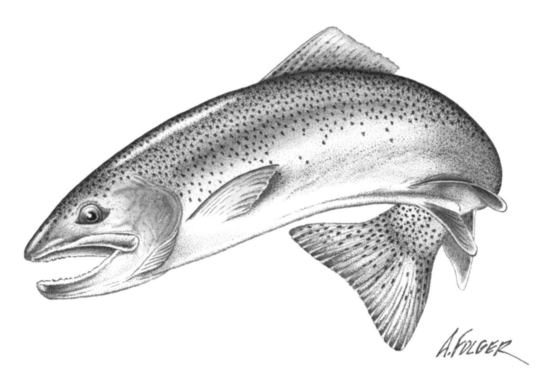

A.FOLGER

Over the years as Slough Creek crashed through the canyon it had cut into the near bank and deposited a nice bed of sand at the stream's edge. Just nice enough and big enough to be the perfect mid-morning napping place for a bull Shiras Moose. As the big guy heard me and swung his massive antlers around I'm sure he was wondering who was this that had the audacity to disrupt his nap. I backed away; he came slowly to his feet and waded across the pool to the far side. I sat there for a good long while before I tried the fishing. The ranger had said nothing about a moose.

# THEY MADE ME DO IT!

Both of our daughters got into camping – well, it was sorta like camping. They each were proud owners of thirty-foot plus travel trailers, and for a few years when the grandkids were young, Shirley and I were able to pull off a major coup. Just short of 14 miles from our home, at the time, was a beautiful little lake and campground, and of all the camping sites available in North Carolina, we were able to convince the girls that this one spot was worthy of our annual Memorial Day Rendezvous.

Cascade Lake

There were a number of reasons why I was partial to the place. First, and foremost, the fishing was good. The water was clear, and the wooded shorelines were free of houses and docks. The separate spring-fed swimming lake was great for the grandkids, and the campsites were clean, bug free, and well-maintained.

Regarding the fishing, over the years I have fished for trout in some pretty special places. I have hiked in, jeeped in, canoed in, and driven up to the banks of some fantastic waters – but I have yet to discover a more enjoyable place, and a more enjoyable way of fishing, than dangling my legs in the cool waters of Cascade Lake on a hot summer day from my float-tube.

Cascade Lake is formed from the clear waters of Little River, which flows out of the DuPont State Forest in western North Carolina. The upper end of the lake at Hooker Falls has a decent population of rainbow trout, and I've seen photos of some pretty nice largemouth that had been caught further down the lake. Most of the anglers are after those. I ain't. No sir, Chad and I were there for the bluegills. As we would watch boat after boat heading out with their bass gear, Chad and I would land one 'gill after another within shouting distance of the boat dock.

At mid-day on Friday, I inflated the float-tube, grabbed my 2 weight, a selection of flies, and headed for the water. That first immersion into the cool waters of the lake, no matter what the ambient temperature is, gets your attention. I eased into my little craft and kicked my way to the far bank, about a hundred yards away. By the time I arrived at the opposite shore-line, the mix of cold water and hot sun had reached the perfect comfort level.

I tied on a little yellow, chenille-bodied, rubber-legged fly, and by the fifth cast I had released three pretty fish back to the depths of the lake. The average size of these bluegills runs around seven inches, and, occasionally, we would catch one of hand size – say around ten inches. Cast after cast, as I kicked my way down the shoreline, the fish were very cooperative. Within two hours, I had managed to catch around fifty of them. Great fun on a two weight.

Chad joined the fun on Saturday, and the action continued, but at a little slower pace. Meanwhile, back at camp, the kids were having a blast with the swimming and the science experiments that daughter Melanie had brought along. All four grandkids, donned in their chemistry lab smocks, had great fun creating fake snow, slime, and who knows what else. It was to be a fun and educational weekend for all of them. By the end of our time together, I would regret some educational parts of the deal, though.

Jacob, John, Gracie, and Grant

On Sunday afternoon, it was decided that our daughters, the grandkids, and our non-fishing son-in-law Jonathan would rent canoes and paddle up to Hooker Falls for a picnic. As they paddled past Chad and me, they had what they thought was a great idea. They figured that their science projects should evolve into a biology lesson, and that Chad and I should keep four fish for them to clean and eat for dinner that evening. Well, that turned out to be a curse, of sorts.

From that moment on, the bite was off. Cast after cast, and no fish. Chad had drifted away from where I was working the shoreline, and he wasn't having any luck either. A couple of casts later I saw a flash of color dart through my sunken fly, and I was hard on to a decent fish. I had seen a few more bass on this trip than usual, and I had hoped that I would catch at least one of them, but so far, they had rejected my offerings.

If I was on to a bass though, it sure acted strange. Instead of thrashing around on the surface, with a jump or two thrown in, this fish headed for the deepest water in the lake. My rod was bent double for a good four minutes, until I finally came into view. Now, I had figured, that with this fishes antics, I was surely going to see a mid-sized channel cat, but nope, it was a bluegill…and a larger one that I had ever seen. As I measured its length, I hollered at Chad to come my way with his camera.

Me and "The One"

As his eyes grew wide looking at my fish, Chad says, *"We gotta keep that one,"* to which I replied, *"No, we don't even have a stringer."* But of course, as the flotilla of grandkids passed us on their way to the falls, after we told them that we were stringer-less, they managed to find a length of wire in the bottom of one of their canoes, and passed it over to Chad, with continued instructions to keep a few fish for the kids.

So, here I sat in my float tube, holding in my hand a thirteen-inch bluegill that I had been ordered by my family to keep. I tried to recall the last time I had kept a fish, much less a bonafide lunker. It had to have been at least 45 years. As the day was growing short, and the fishing had been slow, I relented and slipped the wire through the fish's lips.

The BLUEGILL

The fish cleaning exhibition later that evening went reasonably well, and the fish did indeed taste very good. But, still, I was tormented by my decision to keep him. I did a little research on the average growth rate of bluegills when I got home, and I learned that the fish was at least ten years old…and certainly near the end of his reproductive life-span. That made me feel a little better.

Over dinner, there was serious talk about changing the rendezvous location for next year. Seems there is a great little island off the Carolina coast that has a lot to offer. Supposed to be great for crabbing. Wonder how deep a bend a crab will put into my two weight?

# FISHING IN THE SNOW

Our recent heavy snows have reminded me of the essentials needed to successfully fish our local waters in severe winter weather. All of us have had occasions – perhaps as recent as our last storm – when we had to cancel our fly fishing plans due to inclement weather. Instead of spending a frigid day on the stream we have opted to recline before a climate and resource destroying fireplace and a watch a silly game where grown men throw a ball around in tight pants on television. Or worse, spending the day shoveling the walkway and drive for the little woman.

With proper preparation there is no need for this to happen, especially since there is such a ready source of products available to make our wintertime ventures more enjoyable.

Let's start with the basics.

### Track System for Kubota RTV 900 Utility Vehicle

You will need this bad boy to get you to the stream and to haul additional essentials.

$7395

### Herman Nelson BT – 400 Mirage Desert Wind Portable Heater

The heater should be strategically placed and fired up just upwind of your selected pool prior to entering the water.

$1,900.00 for the budget-minded, on eBay, used.

### Coast Guard approved Mustang Ultimate Ice Rescue Suit

This attire combines the robustness of the Tactical Operations Dry Suit with the high visibility and padding needed in swift water rescues. $946.00

### Electric Pet Deterrent Fence Controller (for your Fly Rod)

The controller effectively eliminates line icing. Do not be concerned with that pesky electricity stuff... graphite fly rods have a very low resistivity ranging from 9 to 40 uqm, which is essentially zero, insuring a relatively safe method of fly delivery. $29.95

To equip yourself with just these basics you have only spent a little over ten thousand dollars, plus whatever shipping costs would be involved. Such a small price to pay to insure a comfortable day on the stream. And, if my math is accurate and you achieve the average wintertime catch rate, that comes to something like an expenditure of, well, about ten thousand dollars per fish.

And, an additional benefit to being properly outfitted: With the noise generated by the portable heater, you will not be distracted by wildlife of any sort. More importantly, you can rest assured that you'll have the stream to yourself, as those without proper ear protection will surely seek other venues.

Regarding tactics, I recommend fishing deep...very deep. And very noisily. As trout, during severe weather enter into a near-dormant state, it is important to wake them from their slumber. As there is little chance that the trout will be in the mood to eat anything once awake, avoid all attempts at "hatch matching" and revert instead to the tried and true "Hellbender." With its weight and broad, deep-diving bill, coupled with its awesome treble hooks, you increase your chances of not only waking, but of actually "catching" a fish.

As a final cautionary note, please be aware that, under such severe conditions, one needs to keep hydrated throughout the day. Many have found that Absolut 100 Proof Vodka is perfectly suited to the task. It is best consumed in a near frozen state, so achieving its proper temperature will require no auxiliary refrigeration equipment.

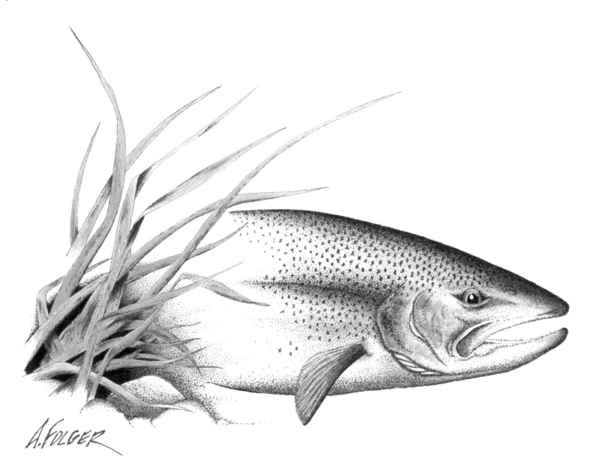

A. FOLGER

# WHAT A DAY!

When I began sculpting trout a few years ago I was in dire need of reference material. At that time I hadn't collected a lot of photo references so I was taking advantage of every available opportunity. I was bumming old issues of Fly Fisherman and other journals from my buddies and I was watching the best of the fly fishing shows on TV. Any opportunity to get more familiar with my subject matter was taken.

One Saturday morning I happened upon something called Fly Fishing Masters on cable. It was a national competition to select the finest fly fisherman in the land. The weekly episodes and the qualification trials were coming to an end and they were fishing that day at a place called Noontootla Creek in the mountains of North Georgia. Kevin Howell (who an hour later had won the competition) of Davidson River Outfitters was in the finals, so the program got my immediate attention. Sure, the fishing was great...but the scenery, the creek...was just as inviting. I promised myself on that Saturday morning that I would someday fish Noontootla Creek.

Fast forward to 2 years later. I was working my booth at the FFF Southeastern Conclave at Callaway Gardens and happened to meet Jimmy Harris, the proprietor of Unicoi Outfitters. From researching Noontootla Creek I was aware that Jimmy was one of the select few that had access to this prime water, so a plan began to take shape.

At about the same time, I was getting started doing colored pencil commissions of catch and release trout and I thought that Jimmy, with his reputation and his access to such great private water, might be able to help me jump start the program. So I reviewed his website once again, picked out an image and got to work drawing. A week later I emailed the artwork to Jimmy›s store in Blue Ridge, GA. Well, they loved it... but couldn't use it. Turns out the fisherman in the photo, unbeknownst to me, was one of their guides... and that particular guide had just been fired! Back to the drawing board.

This time I picked another photo. A photo of a guy that I didn't figure would be fired anytime soon. I picked a photo of Jimmy...and a beautiful brown trout that he had caught on Noontootla Creek. Well, Jimmy loved the final result and I offered him the original artwork...for a price...a day on Noontootla Creek. Jimmy agreed, but under one condition...that he wouldn't "guide." He wanted to fish, and who could blame him?

N O O N T O O T L A   C R E E K   F A R M S
Unicoi Outfitters

So on a future Sunday, along with my son-in-law Chad, Jimmy and I headed out of Blue Ridge for the short drive to the creek. It was everything I remembered from that Saturday morning TV show. The water was in perfect condition and with the fall foliage at its peak. We had the place entirely to ourselves. I, as usual, headed downstream while Jimmy and Chad headed up.

Olive Wooly Buggars, along with a couple of split shot were supposed to be the thing, so that's what we started with. I spent the next two hours drifting them down deep through the runs with no luck at all. I varied the number of shot...tried droppers of all sorts...fished them upstream and down...even put on a strike indicator...all to no avail. Major frustration. Here I was on one of the premier trout streams in the southeast, and I hadn't had a bite! I even (horrors!) tried the old San Juan Worm.

A little later, in desperation, as I was about to tie on an egg pattern that a guide on Big Cedar had forced upon me, I came to my senses. *"STOP Alan! You don't have to do this! Dance with the one who brung you!"*

Yep, I tied on a black and yellow marabou...with not one bit of weight. I was either going to fish the way I wanted to, and hopefully land a fish or two...or I was going home skunked again. It didn't take long. Within just a few casts I had caught one of the beautiful, but small, par marked rainbows that grew up there. And not long after that, when fishing a very narrow and fast run I hooked into a lunker.

When we were gearing up back at the truck, Jimmy had made the comment that my old 1950's vintage Medalist made some sweet music when a fish took off. Well, had he been there at the time of this rainbows first, second and third runs...he would have heard a symphony. Jimmy had warned me about the strength of these fish, and it was no exaggeration. My old Fenwick had never had such a workout.

Two times, as I stumbled my way downstream, I was able to get the fish out of the faster current and near to shore, and two times she caught her breath and took off again. Finally, after what must have been ten minutes, I got her about half way into the net and to the shore. I was praising the Lord...and shaking like a leaf. That fish, without a doubt, was the finest rainbow I have ever caught. I managed to get the hook out and get her fully revived, but I just didn't have the heart to keep her longer while I would have fumbled to get out my camera and record the moment. I laid my rod alongside for an estimation of her length (24 inches) and eased her back into the current.

Chad havin' some fun!

Meanwhile, Chad and Jimmy were having some fun of their own. Chad couldn't get Jimmy to fish though. That man is such a teacher...such a guide...that even though he was carrying a rod, he rarely used it. Rather, he was teaching the finer points of nymphing to Chad (a situation that I'm not at all pleased about, as Chad will now be out fishing me with regularity!) and netting his fish, including the fine rainbow that I've pictured above. From what I heard, Chad's battle was just as epic as mine.

What a day it was!

# IN THE FUTURE

In the future, all trout will be large. There will be no need for huge fly assortments or landing nets because the trout of the future will be a genetically engineered conglomeration of traits that the majority of anglers desire. Their growth rate will closely resemble that of your average six- year-old fed a strict diet of Mountain Dew and Twinkies. Tippets will be out of style as the trout will be bred to ignore line sizes, and virtually any fly that comes close to resembling anything natural will be readily taken.

Upon hook-up, these trout will be programmed to fight extremely hard, but only for a few minutes (determined by their weight), at which time they will willingly come to hand without complaint. They will still secrete a mucoprotein protective coating of slime, but the essential electrolytes necessary for osmoregulation will not escape the reengineered slime layer, meaning that prolonged handling for those grip and grin photo moments will not be a problem.

The days of catching small trout will be gone...especially native trout, as they will be totally unsuited to compete with their triploid cousins. Stream reading will be greatly simplified as all trout will be programmed to inhabit areas free of snags and there will be a pecking order established as the trout line up in their specified feeding lanes.

Where am I coming up with this falderal, you say? How about a 48 pound brown trout and a 43 pound rainbow that were caught in the past year. Neither of these disgustingly fat creatures had to endure the rigors of being born in a stream. Nope, they grew up in Dr. Frankenstein's Hatchery.

These two genetically engineered trout shattered the old world records, and at the same time shattered my opinion of the International Game Fish Association. Just like in other sports, the world of angling has been invaded by genetic engineering and doping. Anything to achieve bigger. Anything to break a record. Anything goes as gene science and chemistry rule the day.

The end product of this tinkering produces huge trout...funny looking things with huge bodies and tiny mouths. The girth on the new record Rainbow matched my own...34 inches. They're created with three sets of chromosomes, making them sterile, and putting all the energy they normally expend in reproduction into body mass growth.

One can only hope that some fool doesn't apply the same technology to the trout's toothier cousins. Imagine the teeth of a two hundred pound Northern or Musky. Or worse yet...twenty ton Great Whites.

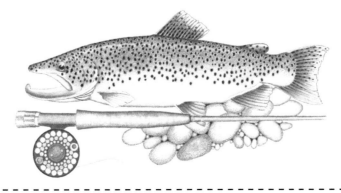

# THE MAYFLOWER

In retrospect, Larry B. was a pretty good fishing buddy. Well, make that an adequate fishing buddy. In fact, if Larry B. hadn't been adequate, and hadn't owned a car, he wouldn't have been a fishing buddy at all. But having a car made him, for awhile, my best fishing buddy of all time. I had heard that there was fishing to be had beyond our little neighborhood –fishing that required a bit of travel, so, *"Hey, Larry B…wanna go fishing?"*

The Mayflower

We called his car the Mayflower. It was red and had those huge fins that cars of its vintage were known for, and, best of all it had that modern, hi-tech push button deal on the dash that you used to change gears. Very cool. And if cars had been equipped with cup holders back then, the Mayflower's would have held a can of ether. No, we weren't abducting cheerleaders…it was to start the car with. A squirt down the carburetor and off we would go. The Mayflower usually got us where we were going, but not without a little chemical assistance. The transport known as the Mayflower was a 59 Plymouth and we would have probably done better using it to chase cheerleaders than fish.

As I said, the Mayflower usually got us where we were going. It was getting home that was troublesome. Take that day after school when we headed for the strip pits. East of town there was an old mining area, and, long before the idea of reclamation came along, these strip pits had turned themselves, all by themselves, into an exotic fishing paradise. Of course, just about anything would have been exotic if compared to our other nearby fishin' holes.

There are abandoned lead, zinc, and coal mines scattered about Northeastern Oklahoma, and the ones we were interested in, if seen from a satellite, would look like a miniature version of New York's Finger Lake region, one long skinny lake after another, each about a quarter mile in length, and separated by equally long piles of tailings grown over with years of vegetation. The "pits," as we called them, were an irresistible temptation to a couple of sixteen-year- olds, and, if the pits had minds to wonder, they would have wondered just exactly what two teenagers were doing there during the daylight hours.

We followed the well-worn tracks made by the Saturday night crowds (avoiding the empty Coors cans as best we could) into the bowels of the place, and through no fault of its own – this time - with a lurching stop the Mayflower parked itself squarely on top of a rise. Business as usual, but we weren't about to let a problem that could be solved later interrupt the present, so we hurriedly retrieved our rods from the back seat and got after it.

The "pits" were inhabited by exotic, funny-colored blue gills and bass the size of – well, the size of – we didn't know. We'd heard that there were monster bass in those waters, but to date, except for the occasional large rise-form, we'd yet to see one. One of the guys that I worked with at the Phillips 66 station when pumping gas on weekends, Dillard the tire-changer, had caught them there by the bucket load . . . or so he said. Of course he said that he'd caught a five pound trout there too.

The water in the "pits" was clear as a bell, but then it would have been, since there was so little run-off to color it. Each of those skinny strips of water were totally supported by the rain that came straight down on them, and perhaps by the waters that bubbled up from some underground cavities left from the mining days. Thinking back, it might have been that bubbling up action that tinged the water a nice light blue and contributed to the coloration of the blue gills. Might have been just as well that we never caught anything of eating size out of the place.

I was armed with my fly rod, and Larry B. had the old steel bait caster with the free spooling Pflueger reel that his old man allowed him to use. Casting poppers along the bank, I was having a blast with the bluegills when Larry B. let out a whoop, screaming something about a big bass. The whoop had an entirely different tonal quality than the one he used for backlashes, so I half-believed him and headed up the bank to see for sure.

Sure enough, he had a bass on, and, just as he was dragging it onto the bank – and loosing the bass - the sky broke loose with the kind of storm that would make an Oklahoma plains storm- chaser drool. Well, it scared the crap out of us and we high tailed it for the Mayflower. Soaking wet, we were grateful to get out of the storm, and storm it did for the next two hours.

You'll remember that the Mayflower was high-centered, so all we could do was sit and stare at the storm and plan our eventual exit from the place. It rained and rained, and rained some more, and we figured that if the tide kept rising, we could float her off just like her namesake might have done to escape a sand-bar grounding. But it wasn't to be. When the rain finally quit we were ankle deep when we stepped out of the car. It would have taken Noah's flood to free the Mayflower from her perch.

We tried everything we could think of to get her back on all fours. We tried the time-tested teeter-totter trick, and she wouldn't budge. We pushed her every which way but loose. We thought of sloshing underneath through the water and mud to dig away the mound that had her suspended but realized that our digging tools consisted of two fishing rods. We finally had to admit that we were beaten so we headed up the dirt road to civilization and help.

Some thirty minutes later we came upon a phone booth, and, as luck would have it, I had some change to place a call – but only enough for one call. By now our dads would be home from work, so we spent a few minutes arguing over which one we'd hit up for help. My dad had warned me about the "pits" a thousand times with some quaint stories about teenage couples disappearing down sink holes, so I wasn't about to call him, and Larry B. just trembled when I casually suggested that, after all, since it was his car, his old man needed to rescue us. He finally stopped shaking when I started looking through the tattered yellow pages for a wrecker company.

Then it dawned on this teenaged brain trust that, between the two of us, we had only two bucks to spend on the tow truck, so that was out. Then it occurred to my half of the trust that Dillard would be getting off work about then, and that of all people, he could find us and he would probably keep his mouth shut concerning our little fiasco. I found the number to the station and rang him up. Sure enough, he was still there, and he agreed to meet us at the car.

Dillard was a bit unusual. One day when the station's hydraulic lift was broken down and he was helping with my *"wipe the windows, check the tires, check the oil, a dollar gas"* routine, he told me he dropped out of school on the day he figured out "cipherin'. He had no intention on that momentous day of his eighth grade year to use this skill to decode the Ruskies' secret cold war communications – nope, Dillard was a bigger thinker than that. He figured that he could figure out, or cipher, just about everything, and such a skill was sure to propel him to riches - which he proved by landing the tire changer job at the Phillips station.

Dillard drove us back to the Mayflower, and, as we sloshed up to the car, he was going on with a treatise on "how to remove a car from a pyramid of muck." Dillard explained that the fulcrum created by the "pyramid of muck" was nothing but a device intended to spoil our weekend plans and protect the girls from our nefarious intentions, and, that, if we were to give him just five minutes he could cipher us out of the mess we were in. As he rambled on about levers and such, detailing his intricate car removal plan by scratching about in the mud with the butt section of my fly rod, Larry B. and I seriously considered borrowing a dime from Dillard, going back to the pay phone and calling our dads. As a tire changer he was OK, but as a practitioner of bovine excreta, Dillard had no equal. So, a half hour later, as he began cipherin' on "Plan #7," we decided that our best bet was just to have him drive us home.

"How was school, son?"was the usual greeting I heard from mom when entering the house, but that was usually well before dinner, and certainly well before dark. On this particular evening dad met me at the door. With a raised eyebrow and a look down at my mud covered Levi's, he just shook his head and said, *"Your dinner's on the table. Where's your fly rod?"*

*"Oh, Larry B.'s got it. I left it in his car. I'll get it tomorrow…if I can."*

# DON'T SHOOT MA'M!

Midway into second grade, we moved to the outskirts of town....new school, new house, and a creek. Oh yeah...a creek. Wild and woolly, through the ages, Joe Creek had carved out the perfect proving ground for three young boys. There wasn't much water in it most of the time, but the carving was deep and wide, full of mature oaks, cottonwoods, and small game of all sorts. Armed with Daisy Red Riders, my brothers and I made the creek our private preserve. Saturday mornings were the best. Rising at dawn, I would pack a peanut butter sandwich, grab my canteen, my trusty BB gun, and head out for a day of shooting. Mom and Dad had a rule about the birds, though. Sparrows were fair game, but don't get caught pluggin' a Cardinal, Robin, or Blue Jay.

Ours was just the third house in the neighborhood and the home set right on the edge of the gorge. Everything on the other side of the creek – that distant land -- was undeveloped. Nothing but scrub brush and oil pumpers all the way to Southern Hills Country Club of PGA fame. Occasionally, we would explore that foreign land, but the creek had too many undiscovered wonders...too many nooks and crannies...too many places just around the bend for us to venture into the oil fields very often.

The best spot was right behind the house. On Joe Creek, a "large" pool was only about thirty feet across and we had one a stone's throw away. Inhabited with little catfish, the creek couldn't have been more than four foot deep at the center. You know how certain smells can inspire a memory? Uncooked bacon does that for me. With our Zebco 33's and a supply of Oscar Meyer, I doubt we ever caught anything bigger than five or six inches. But to have a fishin' hole right out your backdoor, well, it was great, and every time I open a pack of bacon the aroma brings back the memory of that pool and the happy days spent there.

We built forts; we set box traps and snares for rabbits; we even stocked it with trout. That's right, trout. Returning one weekend from Roaring River, we had convinced Dad to let us bring a few live trout home. We justified it by science. We said it was a science experiment...an experiment in survival. Even as a ten year old, I had no doubt that the trout would die in the warmth of the creek, but it might be interesting to see how long it took. We placed three of them in a bucket of clear, cold water and headed for home. After a couple of hours in the car the water was no longer cold, but at least it was still clear and the trout were alive...sort of. Talk about culture shock! I don't recall how long they lasted in the creek, but I'm sure they were belly up before we made it back to the house to get our fly rods!

When in Tulsa, if I have the time, I try to drive through the old neighborhood...and it's sad. That giant house we lived in isn't so large, and the yard across the street where we played football is so small it's a wonder that every pass wasn't through the end zone. The only things bigger are the trees...especially that big Oak right on the edge of the gorge. Mom's Oak tree is about all that's left of Joe Creek as we knew it.

In 1959, Joe Creek flooded. Our neighborhood had turned into a river. Every house that was built on a slab had three feet of very muddy water in it. Ours was on a good foundation, so it was spared. Dad's new '59 Chevy wagon wasn't so lucky. The water was up to its windows and completely covered those gorgeous red tail fins.

Come to find out, Ol' Joe had done this before, so it was decided, some years after the '59 flood, that Joe would cease to be a creek and become a ditch. Our playground was straightened and paved from top to bottom. Gone were the forts we had built, the paths, the hideouts and the catfish pool. The playground of my youth is now only suited for skate boarders and those bicycle jumpin' X-Game crazies you see on TV. But mom's Oak tree still stands.

The day the bulldozers arrived to clear the stream banks was a sad day in the Folger house. To mom and dad, not to mention their indentured servant children who had spent countless hours landscaping our section of the creek, the thought of it being scraped slick and clean was hard to accept.

By the time the diesels were unleashed on our section of paradise, my brothers and I had grown a bit and the lure of the creek had lost its pull on us. Not so with mom. Armed with dad's Winchester .22 WRF Rimfire, she stood her ground and demanded that that one tree be left alone. Whether it was the fear of a round through the radiator, or just kindness on the contractor's part, it doesn't matter...the driver found other trees to knock down.

Every now and then I pull up a satellite view and take a look at the tree. Yes, from that satellite on high, it can be seen...definitely larger, but not unlike it was seen on that long ago day when mom fought to save it.

# THE BASSWOOD LAKE INCIDENT

Once upon a time, in the early spring of 1989, at a place far removed from civilization, four good buddies spent an eventful week fishing the Boundary Waters of Northern Minnesota. On this long-awaited and well-planned adventure there were Jerry *The Mad Cheese Scientist*, Richard *The Ivory Snatcher*, Joe *The Classical Guitarist*, and me *The Speaker of Truth*.

Leaving out of Ely, Minnesota, we lugged our canoes and gear through countless lengthy and grueling portages. (I say "countless" both to elicit sympathy and because I can't remember how many there actually were...more on my memory later.)

Basswood Lake was the destination and Smallmouth Bass were the prey. The weather was ideal, and our preparations were spot-on. With visions of surface busting bass, two of us to a canoe, we paddled towards the Canadian border.

We had been given good advice from our outfitter...the standard stuff like keep a clean camp, hang your food from a tree, and, by the way, stay away from Basswood Falls. What's that, we said? Seems we were a week behind a similar expedition that had ventured too close to the falls. These particular falls are BIG and getting too close to them in a canoe invites a harrowing white water adventure through what must be Class XXIV rapids. Get too close and the falls have you...you can't get away. A week earlier, a canoe got too close and the authorities had given up looking for one of its occupants just the day before our arrival. OK, we'll stay away from the falls.

Our campsite was on a little spit of land dividing two parts of the lake, giving us great vistas and easy access in every direction. After a hearty freeze dried dinner, a well-earned good night's sleep, and your standard campfire breakfast, we made plans for our first foray into the wilds of Smallmouth Heaven. So that each of us could benefit from the sterling conversation and companionship of the others, we decided that we would rotate each canoes occupants on a daily basis. I don't recall who I drew the first day, but it doesn't matter...it's another day's assignment that matters.

Me, Joe, Richard, and Jerry

Well, we were too early for the Smallmouths. Another week and we would have had them. As it was though, we were right on time for the Northerns. Caught tons of them on all manner of top-water baits...but just a few Smallmouth. Every day we sought out a new cove, a new tactic and, of course a new boat companion. We ventured far and wide, and yes, we even headed to the falls one sunny morning. As we cautiously approached the falls we could see, feel, and hear the danger ahead of us. An awesome cataract tumbled down a chute of boulders and drop-offs, each ledge ending in a pool of very fishy water. It was too much to resist. We secured the canoes and with rods in hand we scurried from one pool to the other in search of fish. We caught a good many...and some nice ones too. Don't know what my companions were throwing but I was sticking to top-water baits. Remembering the matter of the drowned canoeist, the last thing I wanted to do was get hung up on the bottom...or anything that might be lurking there.

Days of paddling, casting and landing Northerns can tire a fellow out so on our next to last day, a day that I was to team up with *The Mad Cheese Scientist*, I suggested right after breakfast that he and I hang around camp and take it easy that morning. Jerry was all-in, so that was the plan. A couple of gentlemen fishermen, hanging around camp, taking life easy.

Like every fisherman I have ever known, we had spent the previous days fishing everywhere but at our back-door, so long about mid-morning I grabbed my spinning rod and headed for a small cove...just a short walk from camp...just to see what was there. I had one lure with me...a lure soon to be famous among the four of us as the subject of future fish stories and ridicule.

Back at our home base of Carthage, Missouri there lived two brothers. Two very inventive brothers. They had bought the rights to a unique lure propeller, and, using it, had come up with a lure named "The Woodchopper." Handmade of sugar pine, this top-water bait with the crazy props on both ends was deadly. This was long before they marketed it nationally, so there weren't many of them around, especially in the north woods of Minnesota. In fact, the one I had was a prototype.

The cove was amazing. Shallow and clear with a good number of downed pines stacked like Pick-Up-Sticks just under the surface. As I studied the water, a few of the logs were moving. Good grief...those are fish! Always interested in sharing my good fortune with others, I decided I must run back and tell Jerry...right after I made a cast or two.

The Woodchopper had no sooner hit the water than a "log" exploded to the surface and headed for Canada...and he took the Woodchopper with him. After regaining my composure and cursing my luck, I yelled at Jerry to come join me. But, of course, after the recent commotion, by the time Jerry arrived the cove was vacant of fish.

*"That fish was four feet long! You should have seen him! He was huge!"*
*"Yeah, sure he was Alan. Are you sure he wasn't ten feet long?"*
*"Jerry, I swear...he was four feet long if he was a foot."*
*"The foot part I can believe."*
*"Really, he was! And he took my Woodchopper!"*
*"Well you can get another one when we get home."*

The next day I teamed up with Joe, who didn't believe me either, and Jerry headed out with Richard, who just laughed when hearing the story. Joe and I had an average, mostly uneventful day and headed back to camp. About an hour later, Jerry and Richard returned. As I was helping to pull their canoe up the bank, Jerry started in on me.

*"So he was four feet long, was he?"*
*"Every bit of it,"* I said.
*"We know better, Alan. We caught your fish, and here he is!"*

As Jerry grabbed his stringer and held up a snaky looking Northern of about eighteen inches, Richard chimed in with, *"And here's your Woodchopper to prove it! He still had it in his mouth."*

Needless to say, the campfire conversation that night focused on my uncanny ability to exaggerate, as have most of our get-togethers since. Had they attempted to duplicate the campfire scene from "Blazing Saddles," there wouldn't have been more laughter and finger pointing.

It's been many years since the Basswood Lake Incident, and how they got that Woodchopper I'll never know, because none of them will fess up. But this I do know...that fish was huge...every bit of four feet long! I know he was. I saw him. Really.

# ANCIENT RIVER SMALLIES

Although I lived for 15 years on the banks of the French Broad River, known for its excellent smallmouth, musky - and in its upper reaches trout fishing – I had never wet a line in the lower sections of this ancient river. I say "ancient" because it truly is. World-wide, only the Nile, and another North Carolina river, the New, predate it.

The section near where I lived was narrow, fast, and deep. Filled with snags, wading the river would have been suicidal. Known as *The Musky Mile*, if I had ever been able to con a friend with a John boat into testing it…oh well, that never happened.

So, it's time to head downstream to the lower river. I drove up north of Asheville to an area known as *The Ledges*, where I would begin my exploratory adventure in search of Smallmouth. The foothills farmland I drove through, after even the briefest of rain showers, could turn the river into chocolate milk in a hurry. But we hadn't had any rain for days, so the water was low and clear. It was a perfect day.

I rigged my 5 weight TFO with a bright yellow Clouser and stepped from the bank into surprisingly warm water, which was very different from the streams of my youth. The shoals, mini-rapids, and eddies, although, did remind me of Oklahoma's *Flint Creek* – but on a much larger scale.

I love the way a Clouser negotiates pocket-water. Dipping and diving, darting and dashing from one current to the next, and to my good fortune, two smallies loved it as well. Both were about a foot in length, and in the fast water, they put a good bend in the rod.

As I've mentioned before, rock hopping and deep wading in fast water is best left to the young, so as I had feared on the drive up, my fishing options on this big river were limited. I watched a couple of agile spin-fishermen negotiate the shoals with ease, and, had I not been alone, I might have tried the same. Probably not.

I spent more time walking the trail along the river looking for better access than I did fishing. If I can ever break the habit of wondering what's around the next bend, and just stay where I am and fish, I'll probably catch a lot more. But old habits are hard to break, and, besides, I just

KNOW that the next pool will be better!

# MANNERS

It is very possible that insect hatches, while they are crucial to the survival of trout, may also lead to their ultimate demise if we as fly fisherman do not change our ways.

All of us have been on the stream when a hatch has occurred, and without exception we have frantically searched through our fly boxes, seeking to imitate the particular hatch that is occurring. Once selected and secured to our tippet, we delicately attempt to place our fly between a large fish and the tasty-looking genuine article in the futile hope that we might fool the fish into passing up the real deal in favor of our pitiful imitation. Well, I have determined that our behavior in this regard is quite rude, counterproductive, and that it must end.

If our beloved trout are to continue growing to respectable sizes, they must be afforded the opportunity to eat without distraction. Imagine *your* evening meal. You have gathered around the table with family and perhaps some dear friends, and in through the door rushes a horde of salesmen...pushing everything from warranty policies on the car you sold two years ago to the old *"I have 28 million bucks for you in a Nigerian bank"* scam. Do you think the trout are any less disturbed by these interruptions than we are? Of course not.

If we continue to invade their mealtime with our selfish ambitions, there will surely be a price to pay. I have computed that a feed conversion ratio of 11,623 mayflies to one pound of fish is adequate to sustain the trout's current growth rate, and any interruptions which reduce their caloric intake will have a negative and exponential impact on growth. Of course the ratio is significantly altered if the trout's menu includes measurable quantities of *Pteronarcys californica*. The future is in our hands if we act now.

As there are no reliable hatch schedules for us to rely upon, when we see the water come alive with frenzied trout, we must immediately leave the stream and sit quietly on the bank until their meal is properly concluded, at which time we may resume our embarrassing and unproductive efforts to lure them with artificial flies.

Ignoring this basic rule of etiquette will insure that our streams are full of stunted, and, dare I say...ugly fish.

# LITTLE MOOSE

Little Moose Lake was more a pond than a lake but I didn't care. I was invited to go there, and as teenager by golly, if it had fish in it, I was all for the adventure

The invitation had come from a wealthy businessman who had a cabin just outside of Cooke City, a man who just happened to be a very good friend of Uncle George. He also had a Land Rover and a small boat. This was long before all the Land Rovers were owned by yuppies...back in a time when they were actually driven in the dirt and gravel. This one looked like it had left the Serengeti just last week.

For years, our only mode of motorized transport up into the Beartooth had been WW2 surplus jeeps, so, to ride in comparative luxury was going to be a new experience. He said that the lake was full of good-sized rainbows, and that it was rarely fished. Our nemesis, Erwin A. Bauer,* hadn't been there, so it was a lock that we would have the lake to ourselves.

Little Moose Lake was a short but bumpy ride just off the Beartooth Highway towards Red Lodge in Park County, Wyoming. At about 8,000 feet elevation it looked like many other of the lower level lakes...a very swampy put-in area at the mouth, surrounded by heavy forests...some very fishy-looking shallow water and, of course, some deep drop-offs where the cliffs met the shore.

As we slogged the boat across the muck into clear water, it was obvious that we were at the wrong end of the lake. The air was dead calm and there wasn't a single rise form to be seen. The other end of the lake was another matter. The water was choppy from the feeding trout.

I was placed in the middle of the boat with the oars, between Uncle George in the front and our host at the rear, and was told to head us toward the fish. Having been with Uncle George on many an adventure, it was no surprise that I, a healthy teenager, was invited and given the rowing duties. Fifteen minutes later we were surrounded by feeding trout. A few casts were made and the water went still. Glassy water, with only the reflection of the mountains to hold our attention. Figuring that the hatch had ended, we changed techniques and continued to fish until one of my elders happened to notice that the other end of the lake was now alive with activity. *"Head us back that-a-way Alan!"*

Unlike our first foray, we approached as quietly as we could. Didn't matter. After a few casts the activity came to a halt. I should say at this point that we knew what we were doing...at least my boat-mates did. They had fished these high mountain lakes for years, and they were accomplished fly-fishermen, so it wasn't a matter of incompetence. But this trip was different...these trout were determined to humiliate us, and they were being very successful.

So I spent the next three hours (wishing we had a small outboard) rowing us around the lake chasing rising trout. Finally, it became apparent that we were going to have to change our ways, and I was directed to row us toward one of the more promising shallows. I was completely beat. Four or five trips from one end of the lake to the other had worn me out. I positioned our little john boat within casting distance of the shore and decided that a short nap was in order. Even at that early age, I knew that I would never catch a fish unless my fly was in the water, so I threw that big Royal Wulff as far as I could toward the middle of the lake, away from the shoreline that Captain Bligh and his partner were working.

With my arms crossed over my knees and my head resting on them, I dozed off for a while as they worked the shoreline. By then a small breeze had come up, so I was confident that the boat would drift slowly down the shoreline, negating any immediate need for my services.

I have no idea how long I was out...take a warm sun, a soft breeze, exhaustion and quiet passengers, and it could have been five minutes... or it could have been thirty. Whatever it was, the nap came to an abrupt and noisy end with Uncle George yelling *"SET THE HOOK! ALAN! SET THE HOOK!"*

Dropping a rod into the bottom of the boat is not the recommended way of setting the hook, but it worked.

Fish on! And it was a good one...to date, easily the largest trout I had hooked. He jumped, he sang the reel, and five minutes later he was mine. With already sore arms, it was a wonder I got him to the boat. I'll confess that at one point I considered handing Uncle George the rod to finish the job. What a fish! Probably the finest-looking rainbow I'd ever seen, and certainly the prettiest one I'd ever caught. They guessed that he would easily go eight pounds.

The resentment toward my passengers now gone, I soaked in the praise as we admired my catch. Soon after, they began to catch some as well. As I remember it, we made it back to the cabins in Cooke City the proud possessors of a half dozen very nice trout, which we promptly laid out on the grass for all to see.

As my family gathered around to take some Polaroids, Mr. Shaw, the proprietor of the cabins, came on the scene to let us know that Bauer was in town and inquiring as to how we did that day. *"Better get those fish cleaned and in the freezer Alan...before he gets here!"*

There's a price to pay for everything.

- Anyone of my vintage will recognize the name as one of the more prolific trout fishing writers back in the 50's and 60's. He was notoriously despised by the local anglers as the guy responsible for the growing popularity of "their" home waters, but he was a hero to the lodge owners, outfitters, and others who catered to the angling trade.

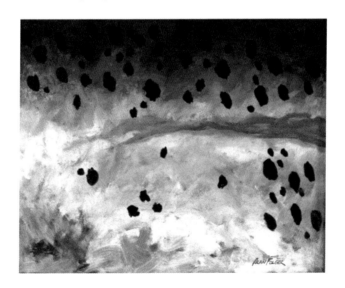

# MARSHALL FRY

There was a time when catching a lot of fish was important to me. A long ago day on one of Missouri's trout parks, Roaring River, to be exact, comes to mind. These parks were the Folger boy's training grounds... close to home and the fish would usually bite... obviously, very important to budding young fly fishers. And, if not biting, there were usually some girls around, bored to death, having been drug on yet another camping trip by their dorky dads.

I had challenged *my* dorky dad to a contest. We'd start at one of the lower holes and fish our way up to the lodge to see who could land the most trout. A small crowd of tourists (there were always tourists around getting in the way of our back-casts) followed us, and, as I recall, we each caught and released thirty-some trout. Yes, we were showing off. I can't remember who won, but it was one of those magical days when the fish were especially active and my hook-set timing was perfect. We caught and released a lot of fish. On other days the fish weren't so lucky.

Back then my brothers and I were under a lot of pressure to bring home the bacon. There was always a good crowd at camp, and we were the designated providers for many campfire dinners – meaning we each had to lug a stringer from pool to pool. As no wading was allowed, we would secure our stringers to rocks along the river's edge, fish the pool, move on, catch one three pools later and spend the next fifteen minutes backtracking to find our stringer among the dozens of others along the stream. Five a day was the limit, so every day we'd each string four and keep fishing and releasing until we had a worthy specimen to fill out our quotas...always under the watchful eye of Marshall Fry.

Marshall Fry was the Game Warden. A wiry little bespectacled guy with binoculars, he was always in uniform and always on DEFCON 1 alert. Lucky for us, his investigative skills and sleuthing techniques were pathetic, so spotting him on the stream was rarely a problem. Fry's duty in life was to enforce the catch limit, especially the "artificials only" and other rules of the stream.

Uncle George didn't like him at all. Arguably one of the best fly-fisherman of his day, my uncle was always on the Marshall's radar. Uncle George was old school in every way. If he was going to go fishing, he was going to bring home fish. Lots of fish. It was a source of pride, but before you condemn him, remember that this was back in the 50's and early 60's...long before catch and release became the norm and *we were* on a put-and-take stream.

My favorite uncle was an enigma. As the long-time Superintendent of Schools for a major Missouri school system, he was one of his city's more upstanding citizens...but there was a rebellious streak inside. Among his so-called faults, he refused to put a nametag on his stringer and one day he got busted for it. The ever vigilant Marshall Fry arrested him on the spot and hauled him off to court in Cassville.

They met the magistrate and a fine was assessed. Always the gentleman, Uncle George agreed that it was a fair amount and that he would pay it...but only after he and the Marshall returned to the river and arrested each and every other criminal who was brazen enough to use a stringer sans nametag. Marshall Fry was furious. He knew that at least a fourth of the stringers would be without tags, and he knew that Uncle George had him. The charges were dropped and the trout dinner was especially good that night. But we knew that our nemesis would pull out every trick to get even. We heard that he was offering bribes to other angles to rat out my brothers and me. He suspected that we were stringing four, returning to camp to unload them, then returning to fish for another four, then another four, etc. At least that was his theory. Now, if we had been night fishing in the off-limits spring lake for the retired brood stock I would have understood his obsession...but we never had the nerve to do *that*.

On another occasion, one of our neighbors that had had about enough of the Marshall's constant presence around the stream, and he cooked up a plan to mess with him. Frank found an empty coffee can, filled it with dirt, and then added a handful of worms to the mix. All that was needed was to be sure that our nemesis could see Frank's plan unfold.

Now, one of the Marshall's favorite observation hideouts gave him a good view of the lower pools, and, sure enough, that's where he was...surveying the fishermen with his binoculars. Frank sauntered to the selected pool, set the can down, rigged up his rod, and reached into the can being careful to sling some of the dirt out as he dug for that perfect worm, all within view of the Marshall. With the worm secured to the hook, Frank slung it to the far bank, sat down, and began a slow retrieve across the pool.

About the time the bait reached the middle of the pool, a siren was heard. Looking toward the Marshall's hideout, Frank saw the dust and gravel fly as Fry headed toward the stream. Coming to a stop behind our blatant law-breaker, he shut the siren down and exited the car in his normal self-important fashion. Straightening his tie and hitching up his trousers, the little banty rooster pulled out his ticket book and walked towards Frank.

Nonchalantly reeling in his bait, Frank acted shocked that he was doing anything illegal. *"All I'm doing sir is fishin' with worms!"* Well, Marshall Fry demanded to see Frank's license...all in order. Then he picked up the worm can with a self-righteous grin on his face, certain that he had busted another of the more flagrant miscreants on his hallowed waters, plunged his hand into the mix, and pulled out a fine example of the injection molder's art. Yep, Frank had filled the can with plastic worms. Digging deeper into the can he found nothing but plastic. Marshall Fry lost it. Slinging the can down he retreated to his car and just sat there steaming. Stifling laughter, Frank continued fishing 'til Fry finally drove away.

There are other stories to be told of our days with the good Marshall, but just know that he led a very frustrated existence for a few years there. However, he gave my brothers and I a gift. That gift was the motivation to lift our eyes from the water now and then...to be curious...to take in our surroundings and be aware.

With the passage of time, it's doubtful that Marshall Fry is still with us. Perhaps I'll see him again someday hiding in the trees along that great trout stream in the sky. If so, he'll be wasting his time, as usual, 'cause that particular stream is bound to be free of all earthly rules and regulations.

# IS IT JUST ME?

Is it just me, or has anyone else noticed over the past couple of years, the number of news stories that describe unusual accounts of fish "fighting back"?

I'm not talking about fish putting up a good fight. I'm talking about fish actually attacking anglers. Bears, sharks, big cats, spiders and snakes...along with rogue elephants, hippos, crocs and gators have been after us for years, and now it seems that fish are joining this hooligan gang of marauding wildlife.

*Giant cod attacks woman in Australia...*
*Tiger Oscar takes a bite out of owner's finger...*
*Lion fish named Lily jabs poisonous spines into hand...*
*Huge Sailfish attacks angler...*
*600 pound Marlin knocks angler to the floor...*
*Asian carp attacks on the rise...*
*A Cambodian teenager recovering in hospital after a puffer fish attacked him in the groin...*
*Girl bather is bitten fatally by barracuda...*
*...and, of course, the normal string of shark attacks.*

Honestly, I don't know what more we could do to lessen their anger. We practice catch and release. We use barbless hooks, and we work really hard to revive everything we catch. Dynamite is in disrepute and gigging - other than in a few southern neighborhoods - is on the decline. So why are they so mad at us? Must we quit fishing altogether? Granted, thousands of years of abuse are bound to get a species riled up, but this doesn't seem to be random. It looks to be organized, and that's a scary thought. Especially if you have the genealogy that I have.

Way back in 1635, the first Folger arrived on our shores from the old country. My ancestors settled on Nantucket Island, and it wasn't long before they started doing what that little slice of land became famous for...whaling. Many of the islands whaling ship captains were Folgers...meaning that they weren't too popular with their leviathan prey. Hopefully, none of their smaller cousins – the ones that I'm likely to encounter – will ever learn of this.

As I am known to frequent ponds and lakes in a float-tube hunting for bass and bream, I am always on the look-out for deranged largemouths. The bream don't scare me...just little pecks...but the LMB definitely antes up the risk factor. And if the pike and musky populations learn of my heritage I may have to begin wearing a chain-mail fishing suit.

# DO YOU BELIEVE IN MAGIC?

A few years back, I had an experience that I would have never believed possible. I went back to Slough Creek after many decades, and I got to share the experience with five disabled veterans and their wives. But we didn't just go to Slough Creek – no, no, no. We went the Silvertip Ranch. The ranch that I grew up knowing about, but never dreamed of actually visiting.

Silvertip Ranch

Situated just outside of the northeast corner of Yellowstone National Park, the ranch is around a hundred years old and is the foremost, leading, preeminent, supreme, un-rivaled, second-to-none, without equal, unsurpassed, peerless, matchless, optimum, ultimate, incomparable, ideal, and perfect destination for any fly fisher.

The owners of this private ranch offered the Trout Unlimited Veteran's Service Partnership, which I was the original Director of, a week of glorious, rustic luxury, and the five vets from across the land and their spouses were invited to enjoy their hospitality and fabulous fishing.

The native Yellowstone Cutthroats were a bit sluggish from the spring run-off. The water temps were in the very low forties, but we managed to catch our share of them. They ranged in size from 12 to 20 inches, and they were gorgeous. We found that weighted streamers were the ticket – fished low and slow, down and across, the crystal clear stream.

Slough Creek

Without exception, all of the ladies – none of them with prior fishing experience – geared up daily and joined their mates on the stream. And those occasions, along with the evenings around the great log fireplace, were special times for all of them. I heard many stories from the vets and their wives, of how the experience was truly life-changing. The healing powers of the water are real.

In spite of the fishing, the accommodations, the gourmet meals, the camaraderie, and the friendships made, the highlight of the trip was honoring the wishes of my parents. My two brothers and I were blessed with parents who not only loved to fly-fish for trout, but were insistent that their boys developed the same love.

From weekend camping and fishing trips throughout the Ozarks, to our yearly trips to Montana, Mom and Dad sacrificed much to see that I and my brothers developed a love for the outdoors and an appreciation for clear waters and God's handiwork. Before their deaths, a few years back, both of them asked that we spread their cremated remains in their favorite stream of yesteryear, and it was my honor and privilege to do just that in the waters of Slough Creek.

Though I know that each of them are fishing the streams of heaven, and their remains were but a visible sign of their lives here on earth, it was beyond special to see their ashes drift downstream on a very special Montana morning.

# CROW'S FEET

*"You can call crow's feet "laugh lines" or "character lines," but these slightly more flattering terms still refer to the same, inevitable sign of aging: the wrinkles that begin to form at the outside corners of your eyes when you hit your mid-twenties. They may show up earlier for people who don't take good care of their skin and later for those who do."*

Those words came from a website I ran across recently, and it was the lead-in to an article on how to get rid of them. Why anyone would want to get rid of them is beyond me. With my rather pudgy and non-distinguished face, I don't have them.

My Uncle George had them, and, to me, they gave him the visage of your ultimate outdoorsman. The lines around his eyes were deep, and were the roadmap of the sporting life that I always wished I could lead. His craggy face and the wry smile that always accompanied it is a memory that I will always cherish.

I've wished that I had them too. In fact, if I were rich, I would astound the local plastic surgeon with my plea for him to create them for me.

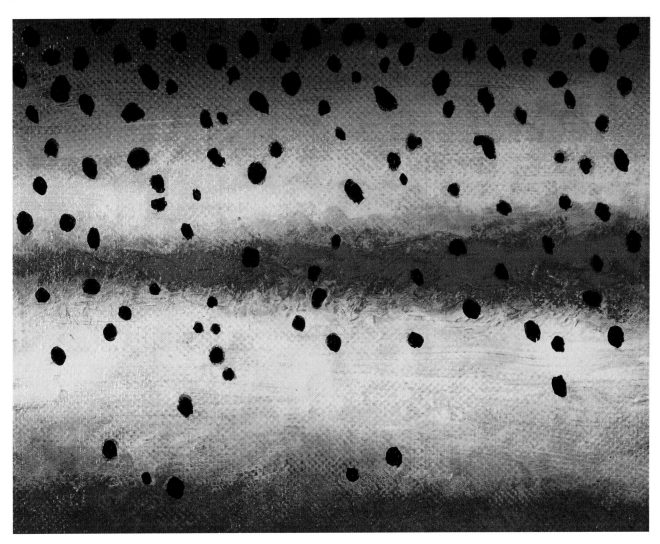

# WINTER MUSIC

Anyone that has ever hunted ducks or geese with any degree of seriousness, has heard about the great hunting to be had on Maryland's Eastern Shore. The town of Easton, Maryland is right up there with Stuttgart, Arkansas as far as waterfowl hunting goes.

Well, this past weekend I participated in a "Train the Trainer" seminar put on by Project Healing Waters Fly Fishing. The event was intended to provide interested volunteers the information and training they would need to organize and run a local program for disabled veterans. Ryan and I have been planning the same sort of training event for the Southeastern USA, so I thought it a good idea to attend and compare notes. The event was held on Point Pleasant, just outside of St. Michaels, MD.

It was a long drive for me, so I was really hoping that it would be worth the effort. Mapquest told me the drive would take ten hours, but they didn't take into account the fact that I would be hitting the DC Beltway at 4:00PM. How do these local people stand it! I spent two hours in stop-and-go traffic.

The evening was dark, cold, and rainy when I finally pulled into town, so I saw nothing of the fabled Eastern Shore.

I awoke the next morning to misting rain and fog. Breakfast was scheduled for 8:00AM at the lodge, and I found the location to be amazing. Formerly owned by the DuPont family as a private hunting and fishing preserve, it encompassed 1,000 acres, with 7 miles of shoreline on the Chesapeake Bay. When I exited my car at the lodge, I heard the music.

While the other guests were bemoaning the lack of warmth and sunshine, (keep in mind that they were all fishermen) I was relishing the atmospherics. As soon as my rental car door opened, I heard it. What must have been 10,000 Canada Geese, and who knows how many ducks, engaged in a chorus that brings goose bumps (I can't believe I just said that!) to a wingshooter. And the weather? This was no "Bluebird Day" with nothing flying but songbirds – it was the sort of day with the cacophony of sight and sound of which waterfowl hunters dream. It brought back memories of the Great Salt Plains that Roger and I used to hunt in North Central Oklahoma.

Throughout the day the sky was alive with birds…birds that continually distracted me from the subject at hand…and birds that my home in Western North Carolina is, for the most part, devoid of.

If I had ever been invited back, I would have jumped on it. But I would avoid the Beltway, and I would have my trusty Browning Automatic 5 with me.

# HALLOWED WATERS… DESERVING VETERANS

The water was incredibly beautiful. Eight disabled veterans and their guides were standing on sacred ground – the banks of the famed Willowemoc – just downstream from where George LaBranche, the author of "The Dry Fly and Fast Water," in 1904, cast his Pink Lady into history.

Not that the hallowed history of the place mattered much to the vets – they were sincerely riveted by the beauty of the day and the opportunity to cast a fly through the feeding lanes of the trout that were legendary to the fly fishing community at large.

The "Willow"

Through the Trout Unlimited Veterans Service Partnership, these veterans were invited to experience the waters of "The Willow" by the members of the DeBruce Fly Fishing Club, whose forty or so members enjoy the peace, beauty, and superb fishing that the Willowemoc provides. Past members of this exclusive conclave have included such respected fishing writers as Sparse Gray Hackle, Nick Lyons, Dick Salmon, Howard Walden, and Ed Zern. Today's guests were perhaps not as notable, but no less deserving.

Some of the vets had enjoyed the sport of fly fishing in the past; some had drowned a worm or two, and a couple of them had never fished before. All were eager, so, as soon as the beats were assigned, they and their individual guides headed for the stream. By lunch time most of the vets had landed a trout or two and all of them had had fish on. The smiles were blinding, and, by dinner time, which was hosted by a local eatery, their stories and the details of their fish caught grew by a few inches…proving that they were all now experienced trout fishermen.

After a good night's rest in the bunkhouse graciously provided by the Catskills Fly Fishing Center and Museum, the vets were in for another treat. Our hosts from the DeBruce club arranged for them to spend the day on the Beaverkill as guests of the Beaverkill Trout Club. With a history dating back to 1872, their club, like the DeBruce club, has a storied past that led to the birth of dry fly fishing in America. The Beaverkill proved to be equally productive to the Willowemoc, and by the end of the day all had landed very nice trout. In fact, one of the guys that had never fished before led the way with four very nice rainbows.

Trout are found in beautiful places, and the mind soothing aspects of fly fishing for trout are known, and enjoyed, by millions around the world. Some describe a day on a crystal-clear trout stream as refreshing - some call it soothing - some say it's just plain fun.

Taking that a little further…imagine that you have survived the horrors of war. Imagine that you might be missing a limb or two. Imagine that you are haunted by your memories, and the guilt that you survived. Putting just one disabled veteran who is experiencing that life situation on the water is better than all of the trophy fish that I have ever caught, or even dreamed of.

# REDFISH

Shirley and I met up with our daughters, Stephanie and Melanie, and their families, at the exotic location of Hunter's Island, just off the coast of South Carolina. This was to be my first-ever opportunity to cast a fly into salt so, I packed my 8 weight TFO and a few of what I thought to be appropriate flies.

In past years, our Memorial Day reunion had taken place a lot closer to home and the fishing was always for trout, bluegills, or bass, so in addition to the change in prey, the change in scenery was really eagerly anticipated. And, the scenery did not disappoint.

Many of the scenes from Forest Gump were filmed in and around Beaufort, SC. The Vietnam battle scenes were filmed right here on Hunter's Island – and it didn't take long to see why. When we entered the road to the campground, the landscape changed from tidal flats to big-time jungle. Beautiful in a very wild and inhospitable way. Arriving at the beach was impressive too. Hunter's Island has nine foot tides, and, arriving at low tide, as we did, we saw about 400 yards of white sand between us and the surf.

A week before leaving home, I called Bay Street Outfitters in downtown Beaufort to ask about the fishing and was able to talk to a guy who sounded very knowledgeable about the fly fishing in the area. I asked about fly patterns and got some good intel on the redfish opportunities. I told him I'd pick his brain further when I arrived in town. So our first stop was at the fly shop.

He wasn't there. He was guiding in Russia, and the help I received from one of his co-workers was of questionable value. My next stop was at a hardware store to buy a license, and the advice they gave me got my attention. The clerk told me that folks had been catching bull redfish right off of the beach of Hunter's Island. That's more like it!

With that information it didn't take me long to hit the beach – right after scaring off a few raccoons that had a fondness for the watermelon rinds left in our campsite by some irresponsible predecessors. With high hopes, I headed across the expanse of sand for the beach. I was fascinated by the patterns the tides had left in the sand. They reminded me of satellite views of sand on the Arabian Peninsula that I've studied on Google Earth from 50,000 feet. A different cause, of course, but the effects were remarkably similar. Okay, so while the saner members of the family were enjoying that other thing that beaches and surf were made for…I went fishing.

The other things

I walked the beach and fished for about two hours, never seeing a fish. So much for the advice I got from the hardware store clerk. I began to realize that without some REALLY expert advice I was doomed for failure. The Atlantic is a big ocean and finding fish in it ain't gonna be easy, so, after returning to camp I stopped into the Visitor Center, picked up a few brochures, and called the one who bragged about their kayak rentals and expert fly fishing guides. I was assured that, yes, the reds were there, they were biting, and that they could put me on them. Chad and I arranged to meet up with them on Sunday morning.

I began to suspect that something was amiss when Lenny, our guide, rigged up a spinning outfit and placed a bucket of fresh shrimp into his kayak. Turns out he had never fly-fished and they had never guided anyone who had! Oh, well, we're here – let's launch these things and get after it.

Lenny said that there was a good weed-bed just up past some docked shrimp boats, so we began paddling north – against the incoming tide. (When you are told that the tide is nine feet, please understand that it moves much like a river. And understand that an outboard motor is advised if you are out of shape.) We paddled for about a mile to reach the designated "Hot Spot", always on the lookout for tailing redfish.

The only signs of life that I saw during our three-hour cruise were some herons, a few egrets, and a guy standing on the bow of a passing shrimp boat. *"Forrest, is that you? Captain Dan?"*

Later in the morning, when we rendezvoused with Lenny, he said that he had caught two stingrays with his shrimp, but Chad and I hooked nothing. The trip back to our launching point – against the outgoing tide –was just as tiring as the morning's trip away from it.

Would I try this again? Absolutely…but only from a flats boat, polled by someone other than Lenny! In spite of the disappointment and the sore arms, the day was beautiful.

# THE DRIFT

It could have been a trout - more likely, the fading light playing tricks through the leaves. Evenings like this mess with the mind.

I was awake before the alarm went off. A normal occurrence these days. Used to be that I would lie awake on the "nights before" imagining the fish I would catch. Half afraid that I'd miss the alarm and oversleep, I'd play fish after fish until nothingness overtook me; then, with the alarm sounding, I'd rise from bed in a manner unknown on days that promised nothing but work. Now, in my seventies, sleep still comes slowly. But for different and unexciting reasons. Yes, I'll play a few trout before sleep comes, but only to pass the time until it does. I miss those nights of eight hours like I miss so many other things that age takes away.

I know this place well and my father knew the spot well before me. He was raised within an hour of the place and he had the good sense never to move far from it. I wasn't so lucky. Careers can be cruel like that.

Tonight, I'm back, and, as I approach the pool, I'm swept away with memories. Dad used to say that there was a big brown back under the trees at the far bank. He said he would never see him during the day, but, in the twilight, occasionally, if the river was really still, he might see his nose appear from the rock, waiting for the darkness that big browns are fond of. He said if I can get the drift just right I might catch him one day.

It's getting darker.

MY FAVORITE FISHIN HOLES

**NEW YORK**
Willowemoc
Beaverkill

**NEW JERSEY**
South Branch Raritan

**OKLAHOMA**
Spavinaw Creek
Flint Creek
Illinois River
Grand Lake

**MISSOURI**
Current River
Big Sugar Creek
Roaring River
Bennett Spring
Montauk
Spring River
Indian Creek
Table Rock Lake

**PENNSYLVANIA**
Spruce Creek

**ARKANSAS**
White River
Buffalo River
Little Red River

**GEORGIA**
Noontootla Creek
Dukes Creek
Callaway Gardens
Chattahoochie River
Flint River
Toccoa River
Soque River

**WEST VIRGINIA**
North Fork of the South
Branch of the Potomac

**IDAHO**
Henry's Fork

**MINNESOTA**
Basswood Lake
Green Lake
Nest Lake

**VIRGINIA**
Big Cedar Creek
Rose River Farm

**MONTANA**
Slough Creek
Soda Butte Creek
Beartooth Wilder-
ness
Madison River

**COLORADO**
Rocky Mountain NP

**WYOMING**
Snowy Range
Wind River Range
Popo Agie River
Firehole River
Madison River
Yellowstone River
Gallatin River
Yellowstone NP
Lamar River

**MINNESOTA**
Basswood Lake
Green Lake
Nest Lake

**NORTH CAROLINA**
Davidson River
North Mills River
Cascade Lake
Watauga River
Tuckasegee River
New River
French Broad River
Raven's Fork
Oconaluftee River
Rock Creek

**TENNESSEE**
South Holston River
Nolichucky River

Printed in the United States
by Baker & Taylor Publisher Services